Beliefs

That

Count

Beliefs
That Count

GEORGIA HARKNESS

A B I N G D O N   P R E S S
NEW YORK   NASHVILLE

BELIEFS THAT COUNT

Copyright, 1961 by Graded Press

SET UP, PRINTED, AND BOUND BY THE
PARTHENON   PRESS,   AT   NASHVILLE,
TENNESSEE, UNITED STATES OF AMERICA

FOREWORD

The purpose of *Beliefs That Count* is to lift up twelve basic affirmations of our Christian faith. Each affirmation is then discussed as it relates to modern man. As these beliefs are affirmed and adopted for personal understanding and motivation, the reader will discover that every area of his life will change. Truly these are "beliefs that count."

This book is not an apology in the sense that it presents all the various arguments for beliefs. Thus the writer does not give the traditional and classical arguments for belief in God. She assumes, as does the Old Testament, the existence of God. Starting with this assumption she then moves on to discuss the nature of God. This approach is taken in most of the twelve chapters. The author recognizes varying opinions and briefly outlines the position held by each. Then she states in greater detail those interpretations that are in the main stream of Christian conviction.

A study of *Beliefs That Count* will provide a fine opportunity for rethinking our basic Christian beliefs in regard to such doctrines as God, Jesus Christ, the Holy Spirit, man, the Bible, the meaning of sin and salvation, the kingdom of God, and eternal life.

The author, Georgia Harkness, has written a provocative book. She is recognized as one of the outstanding religious leaders and teachers of our day.

Appreciation is expressed to Miss Daisy L. Dozier for her work in editing the manuscript.

HORACE R. WEAVER
Editor Adult Publications

INTRODUCTION

THE PURPOSE of this small book is to state the timeless truths of the Christian faith in terms relevant to the perplexities and confusions, the aspirations, joys, and sorrows of modern man in a troubled world. In short, we shall try to see not only what Christians are entitled to believe but also how these beliefs "count" in the business of living.

Accordingly, although at some points it will be necessary to state wherein contemporary theologians differ in their interpretations of the Bible and of biblical faith, we shall for the most part keep to the main stream of Christian conviction. It is inevitable that I shall make some statements with which not all readers will agree. No living person can say, without presumption, that he is wise enough to understand all the mysteries of God. To declare as the sole and final truth a single-track, authoritarian body of belief is not only to commit before God the sin of self-righteousness but to weaken one's witness before men by an offensive dogmatism. Yet this is a long way from saying that we cannot know anything with certainty. Christians do, indeed, agree on a great many things. Furthermore, they live by those beliefs which they hold most steadfastly. Therefore it is to these beliefs that we shall give our main attention.

A word is in order as to the arrangement of material in the book. At the Methodist General Conference of 1952, the first event after the opening of Communion service was, as usual, the reading of the Episcopal Address. Yet it was an unusual occasion, for a significant portion of this address consisted of brief, pungent, deeply meaningful affirmations of Christian faith. One of the most moving and lifting experiences of my life was to hear the late Bishop Paul Kern read these affirmations. They were so simply stated, so profoundly true, so compelling in their witness, that in preparing to write this book I felt that I could not do better than to use them as a framework on which to place what needed to be said.

There are twelve of these affirmations. The book consists of twelve chapters, each introduced by one of these statements. Following each affirmation is a brief discussion of what, in the current mood or plight of modern man, makes this aspect of our faith of special concern. Then there is a longer, though still necessarily brief, elaboration of the meaning of this belief. In short, although in a structure much simpler than that of Paul Tillich, we shall attempt what he calls a "method of correlation" whereby man's existential questions are met by the answers of our Christian faith.

CONTENTS

1

We Believe in God

GOD *is the creative and sustaining Power who works in and through all existing life. God is a Person. His personality transcends our limited human personalities but we are made in His spiritual likeness. He knows each of us and we can have personal and conscious fellowship with Him. God is love. He loves every creature whom He has made and yearns for his salvation and perfection. Not only is His love self-giving, but He craves our love in response. There is no conflict between the justice of God and the mercy of God; both spring out of His infinite love for His children.*[1]

OUR HUMAN SITUATION

Everywhere modern men are *insecure*. This insecurity is economic, political, and social; and in a deeper sense than any of these—though related to all of them—it is psychological.

In America there is a prosperous and, in many respects, an outwardly comfortable state of affairs. Ours is an affluent society unequaled anywhere else in the world. In spite of rising costs of living, salaries and wages for great numbers of people are high enough to afford all the necessities and provide many

[1] "The Episcopal Address of the Bishops," *Journal of the 1952 General Conference of The Methodist Church* (Nashville: The Methodist Publishing House), pp. 155-56.

of the luxuries undreamed of by our fathers. More fine homes, lovely furniture, expensive cars, elaborate country clubs, and well-built schools and churches are produced, used, and at least partially paid for now than in any previous era in history.

In spite of this there is economic insecurity everywhere. Hurry and worry, dissatisfaction, and a sense of grievance are chronic aspects of the world of work. Fears of a loss of profits, unemployment, and economic insecurity in old age hang over our heads. Vast numbers of persons are in debt, frantically trying to meet their payments on houses, furniture, cars, and much else. The keenness of competition in business drives many persons to practices that are admittedly wrong, but which seem so necessary for survival that conscience accommodates itself. Where is God in all this "rat race"?

Every person knows that politically the world is sitting on a powder keg, although this metaphor pales to insignificance when we try without success to stretch the imagination from the familiar old powder keg to nuclear power, which is many million times more destructive. Most persons do not consciously think about this danger all the time; and this is good, for we should be utterly terrified and unable to live with any degree of efficiency if we did. Yet underneath the varied pursuits of work, leisure, and family life there is at the heart of mankind a gnawing fear of global destruction. Again we are prompted to ask, Where is God in all this?

There are many other social dislocations of our time, of which racial tension and alcoholism are the most far-reaching and conspicuous. These and others show themselves in broken homes, juvenile delinquency, and the general unsettledness of family life. Wherever we find such situations we also find broken hearts and frustrated, unhappy lives. Add to these all the normal—or at least the still unconquered—circumstances produced by wind and weather, illness and danger in a hazardous world, and it is no wonder that hosts of people are inwardly distraught in the midst of an outwardly comfortable society. Where is God in all this?

Everywhere today men are *lonely.* There is plenty of togetherness, and the traffic jams on the highways are but symbols of the way lives are jostled until there is little time or opportunity to be alone with one's thoughts. Yet very few people have any real sense of being understood—or of understanding one another—in the inner recesses of the soul. Fellowship in the deeper sense is very infrequent, and this is true even in the family where, if anywhere, it ought to prevail. Insecurity would not seem so terrible if loneliness were not so prevalent. A shared danger, if shared with one in whom a person has confidence, loses half its terror. But because persons are both lonely and insecure, the problem is intensified.

Within this lonely, busy world in which life crowds upon life until only the most resolute can possess his soul in patience, where is God?

Everywhere today—as in all days—men are *unloving.* Not only does this lack of love show itself in the lack of soul sharing, but what is more serious, it reveals itself in sin. Sin is an ugly word that many persons do not like to speak, but it symbolizes a persistent tendency in human life. It is defined in many ways, but at the heart of its meaning is disobedience to God's command to love one another as it is revealed to us through the Bible and supremely through the words and deeds of Jesus. Listen again to the familiar words whose cutting edge may be dulled through sheer familiarity but whose significance has never been superseded:

> But when the Pharisees heard that he had silenced the Sadducees, they came together. And one of them, a lawyer, asked him a question, to test him. "Teacher, which is the great commandment in the law?" And he said to him, "You shall love the Lord your God with all your heart, and with all your soul, and with all your mind. This is the great and first commandment. And a second is like it, You shall love your neighbor

as yourself. On these two commandments depend all
the law and the prophets." [2]

We need not deny that there is love in the world. Nothing is
gained by overlooking man's capacity for unselfish love or
the expressions of it that have blessed our lives. But few
would question the fact that there is too little love in human
relations. It is mainly the lack of love that breaks up families
and friendships and which even invades churches to cause
disharmony and strife. It is a common experience to be aware
of not being treated with love by another, and we resent
being used by another for his own advantage.

Far less often, however, we are aware of our own lack of
love toward others and our indifference to their needs and
feelings. The tendency to self-interest is very prevalent even
among persons generally considered "good." Because of this
fact, moral dullness often creeps up and possesses us without
our being stopped by the signals of conscience that usually
flash before we are tempted to other more overt and recog-
nizable forms of sin.

This happens all the more commonly when the persons we
ought to be loving and helping are in the impersonal structures
of business, on the other side of a political conflict, "on the
other side of the tracks," or among the hungry and under-
privileged peoples on the other side of the earth. Consequently,
the world that was meant to be a great human family "with
liberty and justice for all" is the scene not only of injustice,
tyranny, and heartache, but of bitter strife that may engulf
us all.

In this world of struggle and conflict, of "every man for
himself" and where every great group and nation is for itself
in a vast struggle for power, advancement, and even survival,
where is God?

[2] Matthew 22:34-40.

OUR BELIEF IN GOD

Let us look back now at the statement that heads this chapter. We shall take it section by section to see what light it throws on man's predicament.

First, God speaks to our insecurity. *God is the creative and sustaining Power who works in and through all existing life.*

It is basic to the Christian faith that God is the Creator and Ruler of the universe and of all that is in it. This is stated again and again in the Bible and is the theme of the majestic prose poem that constitutes the first chapter of Genesis. Science may tell us much that the biblical writers did not know about the processes by which God continually fashions an unfinished world, but it cannot go beyond the great truth stated in Genesis 1:1, "In the beginning God created the heavens and the earth." Likewise, wrestle as we may with the problem of evil, the heart of the matter is found in the great refrain of this Genesis story after the account of each "day" of creation, which says, "And God saw that it was good."

There are a thousand ways in which we try in today's language to affirm this faith, but perhaps none is more forceful or rings truer than the words of Maltbie D. Babcock's familiar hymn:

> This is my Father's world,
>   O let me ne'er forget
> That though the wrong seems oft so strong,
>   God is the Ruler yet.
> This is my Father's world:
>   Why should my heart be sad?
> The Lord is King: let the heavens ring!
>   God reigns: let the earth be glad! [3]

This faith has something very important to say to man's insecurity. It does not make life easy, rosy, or free from con-

[3] From "This Is My Father's World."

flict and struggle. But it does indicate a spirit in which we should accept inwardly the necessary uncertainties of existence, and it provides an incentive by which we can change society in the direction of greater security for all men.

In our economic life, for example, it is very essential that we should broaden our conception of stewardship from giving to the church—important though that is—to the stewardship of all of life. This *is* our Father's world, and whatever we have of material resources, talents, time, or energy are gifts from his hands. More accurately, he has loaned all things to us to invest in his service for the making of a better world in which all may share more fully in his bounty.

During the early days of the Protestant Reformation it was believed that the common life was sacred and that every form of daily work which could be presented to God without shame was a form of divine vocation. We have too largely lost this great idea and need desperately to recover it. To the degree that we hold this view, our making, spending, and giving of money takes on a new dignity and meaning in stewardship to the God who "is the creative and sustaining Power who works in and through all existing life."

The faith of the Christian is no panacea to solve all the political problems of the day. To do this requires technical knowledge, responsible citizenship, patient negotiation, and, in the opinion of many, the possession of military strength. Nevertheless, the faith that God is the Lord of history; that even atomic energy is God's energy to be used for human good and not for mutual destruction; that no nation is sovereign in its own right but that God alone is the sovereign Ruler of the world—such a faith makes a vast difference in the way we deal with political issues. To the degree that this faith can be made to capture the minds and direct the speaking, acting, and voting of Christian citizens—to this degree the world will be a far safer place to live in.

Much the same may be said of the other great social problems of the day which precipitate insecurity and injustice.

There is no simple, easy, or quick solution of them. But there is a direction in which to move and an impelling motive to act if we take our gospel seriously. The God who works in and through all existing life will sustain us as we go, even as he judges us if we are recreant to his calling.

Most of the world's evil is man-made; it is precipitated either by "man's inhumanity to man" or by human ignorance or carelessness. Because of this fact, it is not Christian to be complacent. It is not the will of God that children suffer from hunger and malnutrition and grow up in unsanitary slums with lack of proper education; that persons because of the color of their skin are debarred from schools, hospitals, employment, or housing projects; that persons are denied other basic human rights; that personalities and homes are broken through drink and that great numbers die on highways through drunken driving; that marriage vows are often taken lightly and that easy divorces shatter home after home and leave children the pawns of the parents' selfishness.

The problem of evil in such matters is not the intellectual question of why a good God lets these things happen. He has given us the great gift of human freedom and the ability to act responsibly, thereby setting us apart from and above the whole sub-human world. Therefore it is man's fault and not God's design if this freedom is misused. The primary problem, then, is the problem of inducing sinful and complacent people to act responsibly to eliminate situations that cause such evil effects.

It must be granted, however, that there are other aspects of the problem of pain which are more shrouded in mystery. We do not fully know why illness strikes when and where it does; why the forces of nature are sometimes swift and terrible in their destructiveness; nor why, according to our human vision, death comes too early. These are matters about which we must often say with Job, "I lay my hand on my mouth." (Job 40:4.) But there is no circumstance so dark that God cannot redeem it with his presence as he gives us strength to see it through and to find life deeper and richer on the far side of it. So, let us look now at this angle of our faith.

Second, God speaks to our loneliness. *God is a Person. His personality transcends our limited human personalities but we are made in His spiritual likeness. He knows each of us and we can have personal and conscious fellowship with Him.*

There are some persons—both theologians and laymen—who object to saying bluntly, "God is a person." To them, such a statement seems to detract from his divine majesty and to make him too much like ourselves. However, not many are averse to using the adjective form, "God is personal," provided it is clearly understood that his personality transcends our human limitations. Of course, this does not mean that God has a body that can be visualized, but that he is a God of infinite wisdom, goodness, mercy, and love. He is a God of tender compassion as well as creative power. The Bible does not use the term "Person" or "personal" for God, but from start to finish it expresses this idea. It was brought to its fullest meaning when Jesus addressed his God and ours as "Father."

Man is a sinner; that is certain, and of this we must speak repeatedly. But man is also made in the spiritual image of God. Another tremendous verse from the Genesis story of creation says, "So God created man in his own image, in the image of God he created him; male and female he created them." (Genesis 1:27.) It is this fact that gives us our true worth and dignity as persons.

And it is this also that is the supreme answer to our loneliness. It is possible to have an *interest* in inanimate things and impersonal forces, but it is not possible to have *fellowship* with any except a being who can respond to us, enter into our joys and sorrows, our longings and achievements. God is such a Being above all human beings! Although an influential contemporary theologian, Paul Tillich, insists that God is not a Being but, instead, "being itself," or "the ground of being," most Christian thinkers find such a view too impersonal to answer man's deep need for divine companionship.

If we grant that God has made us in his spiritual image for fellowship with himself, prayer becomes possible. Prayer is "the practice of the presence of God." It is communication and response to and from the very Source of our existence— the Source who is also what the late Professor Alfred North Whitehead called "the great Companion, the fellow-sufferer who understands." The familiar words of Alfred, Lord Tennyson then take on great realism:

> Speak to Him thou for He hears, and Spirit with
>   spirit can meet—
> Closer is He than breathing, and nearer than hands
>   and feet.[4]

Prayer is communion with the Father, in whom Jesus found his strength and to whom he bids us pray. Prayer is the turning of our souls to that supreme Source of compassion, forgiveness, and insight who has brought new life to Christians through many centuries of dark days.

Accordingly, the primary answer to man's loneliness today is fellowship with God in prayer. Some would say this is not possible until one has been led to it by experiences of human fellowship, and certainly human fellowship is needed and has much to do with the deepening of the spiritual life. Yet such divine companionship is not simply a man-made thing. In deepest, darkest hours of loneliness Christians have again and again been able to say, as our Lord said on the night of the Last Supper, "The hour is coming, indeed it has come, when you will be scattered, every man to his home, and will leave me alone; yet I am not alone, for the Father is with me." (John 16:32.)

Finally, God speaks to our lovelessness. *God is love. He*

---

[4] *The Higher Pantheism,* stanza 6.

loves every creature whom He has made and yearns for his
salvation and perfection. Not only is His love self-giving but
He craves our love in response. There is no conflict between
the justice of God and the mercy of God; both spring out of
His infinite love for His children.

The supreme quality of the personal God whom we worship
as Father is love. Power, might, majesty, and wisdom to
know all things are his. But it is God's love that Jesus proclaimed above all else. At the heart of the Christian faith is
this great assurance: Although we have sinned terribly
against him and our neighbors through our lovelessness, he
still loves us and seeks to win us to salvation by that love.

God's judgment is real. It must be real if he is a righteous
God, and he would not be worth worshiping if he were so
spineless or so indifferent to what happened to his children
that sin made no difference to him. In short, he would not
be the God of all goodness to whom Jesus calls us to give
supreme allegiance if he were simply a casual onlooker at the
enormity of human sin. In fact, one might say without presumption that even you and I would hardly do that! He who
loves most suffers most at the sinfulness of his erring children and in justice must condemn them.

God condemns, but he does not reject us. Mercy, not
judgment, is God's last word. Around the world are many
millions of Christians who know and repeat the great affirmation of John 3:16. But some of these are not aware that
an equally great truth is stated in the next verse, which says,
"For God sent the Son into the world, not to condemn the
world, but that the world might be saved through him."

Therefore, we should not be surprised to find that "there
is no conflict between the justice of God and the mercy of
God; both spring out of His infinite love for His children."
And if this is true, it is certainly true that in response to his
self-giving love he bids us love both him and our neighbor.

More will be said about God's answer to human lovelessness in later chapters, particularly the one that deals with

our salvation from sin. The next chapter—that which deals with our belief in Jesus Christ—will also speak to this theme. Therefore we shall discuss it no further at this point. It is perhaps enough to say here that as man's lovelessness with its dullness and indifference to human need is our basic curse, so is God's love the foundation of the duty and the demand to love one another.

An ancient seer put this truth in words far better than we can frame when he once wrote:

> Beloved, let us love one another; for love is of God, and he who loves is born of God and knows God. He who does not love does not know God; for God is love.
>
> .   .   .   .
>
> We love, because he first loved us. If any one says, "I love God," and hates his brother, he is a liar; for he who does not love his brother whom he has seen, cannot love God whom he has not seen. And this commandment we have from him, that he who loves God should love his brother also.[5]

And through the centuries men have been reading these words, but often they have not heeded them.

[5] 1 John 4:7-8, 19-21.

2

We Believe in Jesus Christ

JESUS is the Son of God, the eternal divine Word made flesh and dwelling among men. In His sinless life He revealed the nature of His Father and our Father. His infinite wisdom is our guide. His sacrifice upon the cross is our redemption, and His resurrection from the dead is our pledge of eternal life. He lives today, unseen though ever present, and in the acceptance of Him as Saviour and as Lord lies humanity's hope for the present and for the future.

THE QUEST FOR AUTHORITY

Deep within man is implanted the desire *to know the truth.* This does not imply, of course, that everybody has a keen intellectual curiosity. There are many persons who are quite content to let others do their thinking for them! Nevertheless, it was this desire to know and to understand the universe that gave rise to Greek philosophy some six centuries before Christ. It was this quest for factual certainty that prompted Aristotle in the fourth century before Christ to become, for his day, a great scientist as well as philosopher. It also led to the emergence of modern scientific method as set forth by Sir Francis Bacon 350 years ago. Furthermore, it has undergirded the marvelous advances in scientific discovery in the period since that time. Though much of today's science is applied science—the discovery of new processes and the making of new products to satisfy human wants—it all rests on the desire to find out with certainty what can be known about the world of nature.

This quest for certainty belongs to religion also. A person cannot really worship a being about whose very existence he feels uncertain. Doubt is not wholly bad, for it can drive us to serious inquiry. But when doubt possesses the mind and dominates it, faith fades away and persons lose much of the vitality of their religion.

This situation creates a serious problem for many minds. On the one hand, the whole climate of our time is directed toward a trust in science. The popular clamor for more science and mathematics in the public schools lest the Russians outdistance us in military achievements and in the conquest of outer space is a symptom of the common assumption that science has the answer. On the other hand, Christian faith is often defended by repeated assertions that "the Bible says . . ." without any attempt to recover the historical situation in which the books of the Bible were written or to get beneath the surface to find out what God really *is* saying through it. If Christian faith is to be vital, our knowledge of God must rest on firmer ground than either of these procedures.

But the desire to *know* the truth is not the only form of man's quest for authority. He wants to know *what he ought to do*. Life is full of decisions; they crowd upon us daily if not hourly. Many of these are moral in nature. Some are overtly so, as is the decision whether to lie or to tell the truth, to cheat or to be honest, to maintain sexual purity or to surrender to lust. There are other moral decisions, which frequently are not recognized as such. Among them are those that we make concerning the right use of our time, energy, or money; those regarding how to treat persons whose lives touch ours; and those concerning when to speak and when to be silent when convictions are at stake. The very fact that we are created as responsible beings necessitates that we must choose.

Today there is a widespread loosening of moral standards that formerly held society to something like a common moral code. Therefore, to great numbers of people, doing wrong means only doing something at which they may get caught. There are various reasons why persons take these views and we cannot discuss them here. But the net result is this: All the way from the street gang of juvenile delinquents through the free-and-easy sex life of many adolescents and adults to the income tax evasion of many a "respectable" member of society—to do right is to do what one can get away with; to do wrong is to do what is not safe.

Yet, inwardly, people are not really satisfied with these conclusions. Now that older strait-laced ideas are passé, or passing, life has much freedom in it; but in spite of this persons would like to have something to cling to.

This brings us to a third and even deeper element in the quest for authority. Persons want to know *how to live*. In short, they want ground to stand on. To adapt the language of a familiar parable that stands at the end of the Sermon on the Mount, man wants to build the house of his soul not on shifting sand that will crumble and melt away when the rains fall, the floods come, and the winds blow; instead, he wants an edifice that will stand firm amid personal adversities and the uncertainties of time because it is founded on a rock.

Some persons have such stability. They are usually persons of Christian faith, though in fairness we must realize that Christian faith is not the only source of security. But insecurity is everywhere apparent in our society. This is evident in the current trek to psychiatrists, the fullness of the mental hospitals, the frequency of alcoholism, and the appalling number of suicides in America—sixteen thousand in one year. Great numbers of persons, although not "cracking" to this extent, have a pervading sense of emptiness and unrest in the inner areas of life which they try manfully to

conceal. It is apparent that the soul of man cries out for certainty—for something solid to stand on—and too often the
answer seems not to be forthcoming.

OUR BELIEF IN JESUS CHRIST

In one of the greatest passages in the Bible the author of
the fourth Gospel quotes Jesus as saying to his disciples on
the night of the Last Supper, "I am the way, and the truth,
and the life; no one comes to the Father, but by me. If you
had known me, you would have known my Father also. . . ."
(John 14:6-7.)

In the previous section we have noted that the mind and
soul of man deeply yearn for knowledge of the truth, for
a basis of moral decisions, and for foundations for living.
This closely parallels the great declaration, "I am the way,
and the truth, and the life," though not in the same order.
Let us look now at what answer is given in Jesus Christ
to these basic yearnings of the soul.

First, Jesus Christ is the Truth. *"Jesus is the Son of God,
the eternal divine Word made flesh and dwelling among men.
In His sinless life He revealed the nature of His Father and
our Father."*

There is more than one approach to the knowledge of God.
There is the approach through nature, wherein the marvelous intricacy and orderliness of the physical world bespeak
the handiwork of the all-wise Creator. Because it is not the
function of science to deal with what lies beyond the observ-
able world that is open to scientific investigation, science
does not seek to prove the existence of God. Yet every
science gives evidence of an orderly world that cannot be
the product of accident or chance. The uniformity of natural
law, on which science rests, is unexplainable except as the
work of an infinite Lawgiver.

Likewise, there is an approach to God through the moral
strivings of mankind. These are often feeble and futile, but

still discernible as they are unrolled before us in the
pageant of history. Because consciences are often wrongly
trained and have a curious way of accommodating to our
wishes, we cannot say glibly that the voice of conscience is
the voice of God. In spite of this, however, it is still true
that *conscience itself* is unexplainable apart from God. The
fact that some men do deny themselves and take up their
crosses in the service of others without hope of personal
reward is evidence of an other-regarding impulse that marks
sinful man as still bearing in some degree the image of God.

There is also an approach to God through the spiritual strivings of mankind. Paul explained to the people of Lystra, who
wanted to make gods of him and Barnabas, that God in past
generations had not left himself without a witness. Instead, he
gave men "rains and fruitful seasons, satisfying [their]
hearts with food and gladness." (See Acts 14:17). Because
God has been doing this among every people ever since the
beginning of mankind's existence on earth, men have many
times worshiped him without finding him through Christ.
Such gropings after a deity we do not disparage as wholly
false. Rather, we say, as Paul said to the Athenians in the
Areopagus, "What therefore you worship as unknown, this
I proclaim to you." (Acts 17:23.)

Nevertheless, there is a deep sense in which our hearts
respond to Christ's affirmation, "I am the way, and the truth,
and the life; no one comes to the Father, but by me." No
one *does* come to the Father—the God of the Christian faith,
the Father of Jesus and our Father—except through Jesus
Christ his Son.

Science can point the way to the Source of order and unity,
but not to the God of love. Moral endeavor and the impulse
to altruistic action can tell us that self-love brings disharmony
and strife, but it cannot show us love incarnate. Other faiths
point upward in worship, but they lack the clear vision of a
God who not only stands above us but who comes down to us
in love and ever-present, ever-lifting compassion. There were

many "gods" and many "lords" in men's minds and hearts before Jesus came, and there are many today. Idolatry is by no means limited to graven images or foreign faiths. But only in Jesus of Nazareth, "the Son of God, the eternal divine Word made flesh and dwelling among men," do we see God as he really is.

The central stream of the Christian tradition has always insisted that Jesus was truly a man. It has emphasized the facts that he was born as a baby in a manger, that he grew up in a humble carpenter's home, accepted baptism from his cousin John the Baptist, and engaged in a brief ministry during which he taught and healed in a most remarkable manner. Furthermore, it insists that he shared our human lot of hunger, thirst, and fatigue; that he experienced anger before evil and endured agony at the need to die. Some in their desire to protect the divinity of Jesus have denied or questioned his humanity and thus have fallen into the heresy of Docetism, or the belief that Jesus' humanity was only an appearance, not a reality. But to hold this belief is to cut the foundations from under the basic Christian doctrine of the *Incarnation*—the doctrine that "the Word became flesh and dwelt among us" (John 1:14) in a truly human life within the course of history.

Yet while we must say that Jesus was truly a man, this is not all we must say. There are many millions of God's sons in the world today, and many millions more have lived and long since died. There is, was, and, we may well believe, will be, only one *Son* of God. Our Christian faith affirms that in a unique way, which prompts our writing of "Son" with a capital letter, the eternal God became manifest in history in Jesus Christ. In his sinless life; in his perfect obedience to the Father's will; in his willingness to die that men might live in the love of God; in his victory over death through the glory of the first Easter morning—in all these we see that which prompts us to say with the apostle Thomas, "My Lord and my God!" (John 20:28.)

Second, Jesus Christ is the Way. *His infinite wisdom is our guide.*

It is significant that in the church of New Testament times the early Christians were called "those of 'the Way.' " We are told that Saul (before he became Paul and while he was bent on persecuting Christians) asked for letters to the synagogue at Damascus "so that if he found any belonging to the Way, men or women, he might bring them bound to Jerusalem." (Acts 9:2.) To the present, to be of the Way of Jesus Christ is the primary mark of being a Christian.

Jesus gave no precise set of rules for following his way of life. We often wish we could find a verse that would settle all the complex issues of family life, economic competition and tension, international order, and war. This he did not give and it is good that he did not, for in the changing currents of human society new applications of his way of life must be found for each new age. But Jesus did something far better. In his teaching, in his ministry, and in his death he showed us how to live.

The teaching of Jesus is epitomized in the Sermon on the Mount, although it is found throughout the Gospels in his parables and in sayings upon particular occasions which, in their main outlines, have been preserved for us. Biblical scholars no longer believe that the Gospels are exact accounts of the words of Jesus, since these writings were compiled forty to seventy years after his death and thus reflect only the memories and interpretations of the early church.[6] Yet this does not alter the fact that the general picture is clear and that "his infinite wisdom is our guide."

In the teachings of Jesus the key-note is the two great commandments: the call to love God supremely and to love our neighbor as ourselves. This is not a calculating, selfish love inspired by the hope of return. It is the outgoing and self-giving love that is born from our trust in the Father's

[6] As will be explained more fully in Chapter 4, Mark, the earliest Gospel, was written about A.D. 70 and John, probably around A.D. 100.

care. Yet it has high rewards. According to the Beatitudes the "blessed" ones are not the superficially happy persons but the persons who are divinely approved and inwardly blest. They are the persons who, in simplicity of spirit, in comforted sorrow, in humility, in yearning aspiration after goodness, in compassion for others, in purity of heart, in peace-making, and in faithful devotion even to the point of persecution, seek after God and his kingdom. Such living requires more than outward conformity to the law. If we will observe God's higher law, we must not be angry, lustful, irreverent, or retaliatory. We must love even our enemies. In such injunctions Jesus sets forth clearly enough for all time the requirements of the Way—the nature of the God-centered life.

In Jesus' own ministry he demonstrated this kind of living. His works of healing—whether of the bodies or souls of men —were always prompted by compassion for persons as he sought to do the will of God. He could become angry at the defilement of his Father's house and adopt stern measures, but there is no evidence that he ceased to love even sinners. Of his own persecutors he could say as he was dying on the cross, "Father, forgive them; for they know not what they do." (Luke 23:34.)

After a few brief years of teaching and living this message of the Way, Jesus came to his cruel and infamous death which, with the Resurrection, was to embody the central meaning and glory of our faith. In this was to be our life. So let us now turn to look at it.

Third, Jesus Christ is the Life. *His sacrifice upon the cross is our redemption, and His resurrection from the dead is our pledge of eternal life. He lives today, unseen though ever present, and in the acceptance of Him as Saviour and as Lord lies humanity's hope for the present and for the future.*

The cross is rightly the eternal symbol and focus of the Christian faith. All that God was doing for man's redemption and all that Jesus did in suffering love to bring us to God centers here. Though we may not fully probe the mystery of its great meaning, we know that because of it life has been different since the first Good Friday. In it we see how we ought to live; through it God imparts power for living.

To take the cross by itself out of the context of Jesus' total life and ministry is to attach an artificial meaning to it. Yet to think of it simply as the death of a martyr who was misunderstood and persecuted is not enough. We should not observe Good Friday in deep solemnity around the world if the cross simply represented the death of a great, good man like Socrates, Abraham Lincoln, or Mohandas Gandhi. The cross gets its supreme meaning from our faith that Jesus Christ was the Son of God.

The cross of Christ gives us a pattern, a power, and a symbol of eternal love. As a pattern it marks the meeting point of suffering with love, and hence it bids us take up our crosses and follow Christ in fidelity to the call of God. As power it is the focal point at which God has released to men the power to feel their sins forgiven, their spiritual burdens lifted, and a way opened to the new life in Christ. As a symbol it is our clearest evidence and surest pointer to what God did not only for men on Calvary but of what God has *always* been seeking in love to do for his erring children. Because of the life and death of Christ, in which we see in its fullness God's reconciling love, life can be different for us.

The cross and the Resurrection belong together like two sides of a shield. The first Good Friday did not seem very good to Jesus' shattered band of followers, most of whom had run away and all of whom were apparently discouraged and downcast. Then something happened! We do not know exactly the details, for though the accounts appear in all four Gospels and in Paul's letters, there are variations. But the fact is certain. Because the little company knew that their Lord was risen from the dead, they "came alive" with new hope. Armed with this faith and the certainty of Christ's victory over death, they established the church and became flaming witnesses to the love and the power of God in Christ. Eventually this witness was to encircle the globe, and we, today, are the inheritors of this faith.

Rightly we celebrate on Easter God's gift of eternal life. But as John's Gospel repeatedly assures us, eternal life begins here—where we are—as we "believe" in Christ. It begins as we accept him as our Lord and find our lives anchored to God through him. His risen Presence is still experiencd by all those who seek to be his followers. "He lives today, unseen though ever present, and in the acceptance of Him as Saviour and as Lord lies humanity's hope for the present and for the future."

There is much that our troubled, chaotic world needs for its salvation. New motives must be instilled; new outlooks engendered; not a few evil elements in personal, social, economic, and political structures must be challenged and changed. But what our world needs most—if these changes are to take place—is persons with dedicated, joyous, and blessed new life in Christ. It is a life that any may have for the taking. But it costs a great deal. We must surrender all that we have to God.

3

We Believe in the Holy Spirit

GOD manifests Himself upon the scene of our daily living as the Lord and Giver of life: interpreting the divine will to our human hearts, comforting us in our sore bereavements, awakening within us a hunger for the eternal, quickening our souls to repentance for sin, witnessing with our spirits that we are the children of God. The nature of the Holy Spirit often lies beyond the limits of our knowledge and understanding, but the glorious fact of His presence in our minds and hearts is the central certainty of our Christian experience.

MAN'S HUNGER FOR GUIDANCE, COMFORT, AND STRENGTH

There is nothing new about man's spiritual hungers. They are as old as mankind. In many respects both primitive religion and the quest for spiritual power and peace that underlies the other non-Christian religions give evidence of it. So deep-seated is this correlation between religion and man's spiritual hungers that some persons would say that religion as a whole is simply a projection of man's own ego and its impulses—an unconscious desire to find comfort in an uncomfortable world.

We do not need to make this the sole explanation of the existence of religion, however. The Christian who believes in the objective revelation of God in Jesus Christ will not be content with any subjective explanation that denies or minimizes God's taking the initiative in love for man's salvation. Nevertheless, God has made us with these deep hungers, and they must be satisfied or life flounders in confusion and despair.

Man has always been thus hungering—and floundering. But because of the great complexity of our world today, man feels his own inadequacy more than ever before. There is a paradox here, for today, more than ever, man trusts not only in the physical sciences but also in scientific education for character building. He also depends upon social case work, upon vocational guidance and other forms of counseling, and, when all these fail, upon psychiatry to bring adjustment to maladjusted personalities. We must repeat that none of these pursuits should be disparaged. We may well believe God wants us to use the best knowledge and intelligence that we possess, and to do this, we must use these channels of help where they are needed and available. Yet the ultimate answer to man's hunger for guidance, for comfort, and for strength is found in none of these. There are deep hungers that must be satisfied elsewhere.

The satisfaction of man's deepest needs is found in the intimate, immanent presence of God as the living Christ and as the Holy Spirit. In the third affirmation of faith found in *The Methodist Hymnal* (the so-called Korean Creed) are these words:

> We believe in the Holy Spirit, God present with us
> for guidance, for comfort and for strength.[7]

That says it! The final answer to our need is God present with us in all our perplexities, troubles, and times of weakness. And this is what we mean by God as Holy Spirit. But now let us look further at this element of our faith.

[7] *The Methodist Hymnal,* p. 512.

OUR BELIEF IN THE HOLY SPIRIT

What does the Holy Spirit do? We shall not attempt to answer this question abstractly but in terms of the difference the Holy Spirit makes. Our initial statement tells us this in phrase after phrase. Therefore, we must look at it again.

God manifests Himself upon the scene of our daily living as the Lord and Giver of life: interpreting the divine will to our human hearts, comforting us in our sore bereavements, awakening within us a hunger for the eternal, quickening our souls to repentance for sin, witnessing with our spirits that we are the children of God.

THE HOLY SPIRIT AS INTERPRETER AND GUIDE

We noted in the previous chapter how hard it is to know the will of God in specific matters of daily decision. Neither the words of Jesus nor the voice of the Holy Spirit will give us any rule of thumb, any automatic or legalistically precise answers. Having prayed earnestly for light, we must still seek it. We must use the best wisdom of our minds as well as the devotion of our hearts.

But what a difference the Holy Spirit makes when we pray earnestly and listen receptively! The difference may not be apparent all at once. Perhaps most of those who will read these words will have had times when they felt sure that God was speaking to them in some great service of worship, through the voice of a modern prophet, or in some soul-stirring personal experience. Yet most of us have also had other times when we were not sure. We have tried to pray and have found no response, or we have felt a compelling impulse which we have suspected might be the clamor of our own desires.

How then can we know when the Spirit speaks? There is no blueprint or precise set of rules to follow, but there are several signposts that will carry us far.

The first of these is "the mind of Christ." "Have this mind among yourselves," says Paul, "which you have in Christ Jesus."

If anything that we *think* is the voice of the Holy Spirit prompts us to spite, to unkind words or acts, or to self-righteousness, we may be sure it is *not* God's voice! The more we know about Jesus as he is revealed to us through the New Testament and in our daily companionship with Christ, the more clearly and potently the Spirit moves us to faith and love.

A second directive is suggested by the account of the coming of the Holy Spirit at Pentecost. What does this tell us about conditions under which the Holy Spirit works?

The Holy Spirit came to the first Christians when they were in a receptive mood and were waiting for it. And it had the effect of prompting them to share not only their prayers and praise, but their possessions—even their daily bread. Furthermore, it came not to each one in isolation, but in a fellowship.

Today the natural channel for the witness of the Spirit is the Church, but not simply the church as a large and highly organized institution. The Holy Spirit speaks where Christians in churches listen for God's voice above the clamor of the world, accept the obligations of discipleship, and reinforce one another in love.

In many instances where difficult decisions have had to be made, the best counsel has come through corporate listening to God and a corporate sharing of deep concerns in the spirit of loving service. The experience of the Quakers is a good example.

Finally, an indispensable requirement for having the witness of the Spirit is the spirit of willing obedience. It is reported that Jesus replied to those who questioned his authority, "If any man's will is to do his [the Father's] will, he shall know whether the teaching is from God. . . ." (John 7:17.)

The Holy Spirit as Comforter

In the King James Version of the Bible John says that
Jesus spoke the following words to the Twelve in his fare-
well address in the upper room:

> These things have I spoken unto you, being yet
> present with you.
> But the Comforter, which is the Holy Ghost, whom
> the Father will send in my name, he shall teach you
> all things, and bring all things to your remembrance,
> whatsoever I have said unto you.[8]

The Revised Standard Version not only translates "Holy
Ghost" as "Holy Spirit," but it also translates "the Com-
forter" as "the Counselor." This is a more accurate translation, which we would do well to follow. But the change in
wording does not alter the fact that the Holy Spirit is not
only a counselor—as we saw in the last section—but a com-
forter as well.

How often we have heard Christians say after some deep
bereavement or other trouble, "I could not have taken it if
the Lord had not seen me through it!" This simple statement
speaks for many of us. But so also do the great, familiar
words of Paul with which he opens the Second Letter to
the Corinthians:

> Blessed be the God and Father of our Lord Jesus
> Christ, the Father of mercies and God of all comfort,
> who comforts us in all our affliction, so that we may
> be able to comfort those who are in any affliction,
> with the comfort with which we ourselves are com-
> forted by God. For as we share abundantly in Christ's
> sufferings, so through Christ we share abundantly in
> comfort too.[9]

[8] John 14:25-26.
[9] 2 Corinthians 1:3-5.

We shall not speak more upon this theme, for one who has passed through deep waters and experienced this comfort will need no elaboration of its meaning. Furthermore, others who have never felt this comfort could scarcely grasp its greatness. It is enough to say that, without it, life at many points would be stark and terrible. With it there is a joy that can transcend pain and renew life.

The English preacher of a generation ago, G. A. Studdert-Kennedy, put this truth in unforgettable words when he wrote:

> Peace does not mean the end of all our striving,
>   Joy does no mean the drying of our tears;
> Peace is the power that comes to souls arriving
>   Up to the light where God himself appears.[10]

THE HOLY SPIRIT AS QUICKENER AND LIFE-GIVER

Our initial statement affirms that God manifests himself "as the Lord and Giver of life: . . . awakening within us a hunger for the eternal, quickening our souls to repentance for sin." Although the Father, the Son, and the Holy Spirit are one God, each has been considered as having a special relationship.

Traditionally, the Father has been thought of as the Creator, Christ as the Redeemer, and the Holy Spirit as the Sanctifier and Life-giver. This means that the same God who gave us life in the beginning gives newness of life through Christ and builds us up in it through the Holy Spirit. We are not sanctified to perfect sinlessness; that belongs only to Jesus Christ. If we assume that we can be perfectly sinless, the term "sanctification" takes on a dangerous tinge of self-righteousness. Nevertheless, we can be—and ought to be—sanctified by the Holy Spirit in the sense that we are en-

---

[10] From "The Suffering God" in *The Unutterable Beauty* (New York: Harper & Brothers, Publishers, 1936), p. 4. Used by permission.

abled to "grow in the grace and knowledge of our Lord and Savior Jesus Christ." (2 Peter 3:18.)

We are tempted to think we can grow to spiritual maturity by our own devising. But we are likely to come to the same conclusion that Paul reached when he said, "I do not understand my own actions. For I do not do what I want, but I do the very thing I hate. . . . I can will what is right, but I cannot do it." (Romans 7:15, 18b.) Only God's grace can speak to our futility and sin. Yet this grace, which is the gift of God to conquer sin, is not simply thrust upon us; it must be sought with an openness of spirit and a hunger of the soul. It is at this point that the work of the Holy Spirit, "awakening in us a hunger for the eternal," becomes manifest. Both initially and all the way in our Christian pilgrimage the Holy Spirit spurs and leads us on. It never coerces or drags us to submission against our wills. But it does speak to us ever insistently in the manner portrayed by Francis Thompson in his great poem "The Hound of Heaven."

If we would go forward in the Christian life, there is one step we *must* take. This requirement is repentance. This is not the same as a tangled guilt complex that is more properly called remorse. Instead, repentance means true contrition—an eagerness to seek the Father's forgiveness and a willingness to "bring forth fruits meet for repentance." We must repent not once, but many times; for life is a continuing battle against sin even after its power has been broken by the divine mercy and forgiveness. In the famous words of Martin Luther, the Christian is *simul justus et peccator* (at the same time justified and a sinner). And in this quickening of the soul to repentance the Holy Spirit speaks.

THE HOLY SPIRIT AS WITNESS

The emphasis on the witness of the Spirit in Methodism arises from John Wesley's recognition of the central importance of Christian experience. Neither the sacraments of the church nor right doctrines can save a man from sin or bring him into a living fellowship with God in Christ. Only a change of heart can do this.

It is only when we "truly and earnestly repent of our sins" and intend, by the power of God, to lead a new life that the miracle of the new birth transforms us and gives us assurance of salvation. And such assurance we need not lack, for it is "the Spirit himself bearing witness with our spirit" that enables us to know that the Father has received us as his children and has set us upon a new course.

Although the witness of the Spirit as an assurance of salvation was central to Wesley and is also important for us, it is apparent from what has already been said that no Christian ought to be "at ease in Zion" in his assurance of salvation. Salvation is not a once-and-for-all, static process. Instead, the new birth must be followed by growth in love and by holiness in living. The Holy Spirit not only witnesses to the change wrought within us but it also quickens us to repentance and to action in daily decisions and duties.

THE HOLY SPIRIT—POWER OR PERSON?

There is much we can agree upon concerning the nature and work of the Holy Spirit without raising the issue implied in the question above. Therefore we have left this discussion until now. But we ought not to bypass it entirely.

The nature of the Holy Spirit often lies beyond the limits of our knowledge and understanding, but the glorious fact of His presence in our minds and hearts is the central certainty of our Christian experience.

It is interesting to notice that the personal pronoun "His" is used in this statement. But is this necessary? The Bible itself presents two points of view concerning this question. Therefore let us look further at the biblical foundations of this doctrine.

In the Old Testament there are numerous references to the Spirit of God, such as the great passage "Whither shall I go from thy Spirit?" (Psalm 139:7a.) It is also interesting to note that in this context the word "Spirit" means "God present" and "God acting." In most of these passages we find no adjective before the word "Spirit," and in the familiar prayer of Psalms 51:11,

> "Cast me not away from thy presence,
>   and take not thy holy Spirit from me,"

the word "holy" is simply an adjective and is written with a small "h."

In the New Testament, however, we find that the term "Holy Spirit" refers not only to the Spirit of God but also to the presence of the living Christ.

It is significant that in the earliest New Testament writings—the Letters of Paul—the terms "Holy Spirit," "the Spirit of God," "the Spirit of Jesus Christ," or simply "Christ," "the Lord," or "the Spirit" are used interchangeably. This identification becomes complete in 2 Corinthians 3:17, which says, "Now the Lord is the Spirit."

Without getting into the intricate controversies that came a little later in the church, Paul, from experience as a Christian, could think of "the Lord" as God, as Jesus Christ, or as the Holy Spirit. And so can we.

Therefore we ask, Is the Holy Spirit "he" or "it"? Such passages as these would certainly prompt us to use the same pronoun as we would for God or Christ, and this is reinforced by the baptismal formula of Matthew 28:19 and the apostolic benediction of 2 Corinthians 13:14. In the Last Supper discourse, which promises that upon our Lord's going away "the Counselor, the Holy Spirit," will be sent in his name, the reference is decidedly personal.

However, there are other passages—both in John's Gospel and in Acts—in which the Holy Spirit is referred to as the *gift* of God, much as we might speak of God's grace or power. The Holy Spirit thus came upon Jesus at his baptism and upon the disciples on the day of Pentecost.

It is promised that the heavenly Father, with a greater love than that of an earthly parent, will give the Holy Spirit to those who ask him. Jesus and others in various passages are said to have been "filled with the Holy Spirit."

Therefore, we may properly speak of the Holy Spirit either as "he" or "it." The pronoun to be used depends on whether what we want to stress is the unity of the Holy Spirit with God in Christ or the gift of God's presence for guidance, comfort, and strength.

So here we had better let the matter rest. There is no real contradiction between the Holy Spirit as God himself and as his gift to us of guidance, grace, and power for every need. The context in which we speak determines the pronoun that we use. And though we may never fathom the full mystery of God's nature as Father, Son, and Holy Spirit, we still can know the glorious fact of his presence in our minds and hearts.

Amid the conditions of our confused world wherein many discordant voices blare and earthly wisdom often seems inadequate, is anything more needed?

We Believe in the Bible

*T HE Scriptures are the record of God's progres-
sive revelation of Himself through inspired men,
and the story of His righteous purpose in history
to bring mankind to final perfection in Christ. The
Bible contains all that God requires for salvation
and is the sufficient rule of both faith and conduct.
It has withstood all efforts to destroy it; it has survived the scientific study of its pages, and by its
enduring truth it has confounded its critics and stands
today more historically credible and more spiritually
indispensable than ever before. It is God's eternal
Word to every generation.*

How Can We Know?

As was indicated in chapter two, there is in modern man
a deep-seated hunger to know what he can believe about
God and God's ways with the world. Man gropes about in
the dark seeking ground to stand on.

With some this outreach takes the form of a new interest
in the Bible. This is not true of all persons and is probably
not true of the majority of those in the churches, to say
nothing of those outside. Yet enough persons want to know
what they can believe about the Bible and its message about
God that biblical movies are often major box-office successes,
and any television dramatization of biblical scenes usually

secures good viewing. This is not to suggest that such portrayals have spiritual interest only, for often sex themes and other devices to catch attention are woven into such productions. But that a biblical groundwork should be presented at all is tacit evidence that the public is concerned.

Regardless of these facts, however, there is a vast amount of biblical illiteracy abroad in the land. This is due in a large part to our idea of the separation of church and state. This concept has kept instruction in the world's greatest literary masterpiece and its most influential body of literature out of the public schools and hence out of the primary channel for the transmission of our cultural heritage. It is also due to the facts that church schools have not been as good as they should have been and that neither the church nor the home has taught the Bible to a degree that is at all comparable with its importance. Even where it has been taught, the full sweep and depth of its meaning has often been lost and perversions of its truth introduced. A good example of this situation is found in some conservative churches where great emphasis is placed upon quoting and memorizing verses regardless of their contexts.

Yet the time is ripe for a discovery—or a rediscovery—of the great message of the Bible. Theology today is mainly biblical theology. Christian education in the church schools is doing a better job than ever in the past, and great numbers of adult minds are open and eager to learn what the Bible has to say. Therefore we ask, What *does* it say?

The Bible as a Record of Revelation

The scriptures are the record of God's progressive revelation of Himself through inspired men, and the story of His righteous purpose in history to bring mankind to final perfection in Christ.

The first observation that we make concerning this statement is that it does not claim that the Bible itself is an in-

fallible revelation. It is the *record* of revelation. It is the story
told in many forms of writing and by men of many centuries
concerning the way in which God moved in the affairs of men
and led them onward to the full expression of his purpose
in his Son. It was written by inspired men, but this does
not mean that God inspired them in any mechanical or automatic fashion such as that of dictating, word for word, what
they should write. They lived as children of their times, not
perfectly wise or perfectly good, and not able fully to divest
themselves of ideas that were prevalent in their day. Ex-
amples of this fact can be found in references to the legitimacy
of polygamy in the Old Testament and of slavery in both
Old and New Testaments. Yet in spite of these limitations
the writers of the Bible had some most remarkable insights
concerning the nature of God and how he was seeking to
bring his erring children to fuller obedience to his holy will.

Inspiration means "inbreathing." The Bible certainly contains the breath of God within it, even though it comes to
us through fallible human channels. We need to read it in
the mood of the familiar hymn:

> Breathe on me, Breath of God,
>   Fill me with life anew,
> That I may love what Thou dost love,
>   And do what Thou wouldst do.[11]

When we do this, the Bible becomes for us the Word of
God—"God's eternal Word to every generation."

Whether we should call the Bible the record of God's
progressive revelation depends on the meaning we put into
the word "progressive." This term has somewhat gone out
of vogue in theological circles today because it suggests a
steady evolutionary advance. There were, in fact, many ups
and downs in Israel's discernment of the nature and purpose
of God, and the New Testament is not all of one steadily

[11] By Edwin Hatch.

advancing upward trend. Nevertheless, if we take the term "progressive" to mean only that God disclosed himself to men in relation to their world as fast but no faster than they were able to grasp his purposes and their meanings, the term is appropriate enough. It was "in the fullness of time," not immediately upon creation or in the early stages of Old Testament history, that the highest disclosure in Christ with the establishment of his Church to perpetuate the gospel was given. What we have in the Bible is the record of this upward climb to fuller discernment of God's supreme purpose in history.

THE BIBLE AS BASIS OF FAITH AND CONDUCT

The Bible contains all that God requires for salvation and is the sufficient rule of both faith and conduct.

In a sense the above statement is profoundly true. Yet we must be careful not to misunderstand it or to oversimplify it. To do so is to contradict the very idea it aims to present to us.

What God requires above all else for salvation is our acceptance of Jesus Christ as our Lord and Savior, our repentance for sin, our moral obedience to his call, and our willingness to try to love God and our neighbor with the full dedication of our lives. This is all in the Bible, for the New Testament repeatedly sets forth this message. For this reason we can say that the Bible "contains all that God requires for salvation."

Yet trouble enters when we quote verses here and there and put meanings on them which are not supported either by the total message of Jesus or by the facts of our own experience. For example, Jesus said to the rich young ruler, "Go, sell what you have, and give to the poor, and you will have treasure in heaven; and come, follow me." (Mark 10:21.) This does not mean that we must literally sell all that we have and distribute it to the poor, thus becoming penniless in order to be followers of Jesus. Nor is this command irrelevant in a possession-centered world! It is between these two interpretations that we must find our duty in our day.

This illustrates also how to take the statement that the Bible is "the sufficient rule of both faith and conduct." It gives us the basis on which both Christian faith and Christian practice must be grounded. This foundation is the revelation of God in Jesus Christ, of which we have knowledge through the Bible. On what we find in the Bible all the great truths of the Christian faith are grounded. This is where we gain our knowledge of God as Creator and Ruler of the world; our concept of him as loving Judge and Redeemer of men; our belief that Jesus Christ is his Son and our Lord and Savior; and the idea that the Holy Spirit is our ever-present Guide and divine Companion.

Yet these are truths with a profound and vital meaning for faith and conduct. They are not rules. The Bible as a whole—including even the words recorded as spoken by Jesus—gives us little in the way of rules. To try to make specific rules out of eternal principles is to distort the Bible's message. Even the Ten Commandments, given in the setting of early Hebrew society but still relevant today, have to be applied in the light of contemporary circumstances. When we look at such great New Testament passages as the Sermon on the Mount or the thirteenth chapter of First Corinthians, we get the general impact, but we find that we still must make the application. To literalize such passages as "Give to him who begs from you, and do not refuse him who would borrow from you" (Matthew 5:42) and to make these injunctions a rule for all time would soon not only impoverish us but would disrupt society. Paul states well our aim: "Have this mind among yourselves, which you have in Christ Jesus." (Philippians 2:5.) In doing this we will find the foundation of both faith and practice.

To give one more example, we may ask, What does the Bible say about prayer? It enjoins throughout its scope the worship of God and the approach to God in prayer. Indeed, some of the greatest devotional poetry of all time is found in the Hebrew psalms. The mission and ministry of Jesus were undergirded by prayer; and Jesus not only taught his followers what they should pray for, but he set before them the supreme example. What, then, do we make of such words as these: "Truly, I say to you, whoever says to this mountain, 'Be taken up and cast into the sea,' and does not doubt in his heart, but believes that what he says will come to pass, it will be done for him. Therefore I tell you, whatever you ask in prayer, believe that you receive it, and you will" (Mark 11:23-24)?

Again and again persons have prayed with deep faith for the removal of mountains of ill health or other trouble and the request has not been granted. Are we to say that lack of faith was the only barrier? Apparently this was not the case with Paul, whose thorn in the flesh was not removed in response to prayer (2 Corinthians 12:7-10). Instead of pinning our faith to particular verses and possibly having it crash because of unfulfilled expectations, we might better find our total support where Jesus found it—in the loving care of the Father and in trust of God's presence even in the midst of trouble.

The illustrations cited show the dangers in "proof-texting," which is a very common misuse of the Bible. Yet we must emphasize that the Bible in its deeper meanings is revelant to every human situation and gives us all we need as the foundation for living. Although we must guard against supposing that the Bible gives all the answers, we must not forget that the kind of God, the nature of Christ, and the way of living which the Bible sets forth is what the world needs most, today and always. Because of this fact we can confidently say that the Bible is "God's eternal Word to every generation."

THE BIBLE AND ITS CRITICS

It has withstood all efforts to destroy it; it has survived the scientific study of its pages, and by its enduring truth it has confounded its critics and stands today more historically credible and more spiritually indispensable than ever before. It is God's eternal Word to every generation.

Another topic we should discuss is the meaning of biblical criticism. This is an ambiguous term with a number of meanings. Failure to see this fact has caused much misunderstanding and sometimes even hard feelings and unchristian attacks that could have been avoided by better understanding.

One use of the word "criticism" is its ordinary meaning—fault-finding, picking flaws, and harsh judgment with which is often joined the barbs of ridicule. When we criticize another person, a television program, or a book, or when we criticize how one dresses, does his work, or drives a car, we usually pass an adverse judgment. Doing this is such an ever-present tendency of human nature that Jesus felt impelled to say in the Sermon on the Mount, "Judge not, that you be not judged. For with the judgment you pronounce you will be judged, and the measure you give will be the measure you get." (Matthew 7:1-2.)

The Bible has sometimes been critized in this same sense. To critics of this type its stories sound like quaint old myths that are rather interesting vestiges of a primitive society but of no particular significance. To them the Bible seems to be full of miracle stories which have much to say that cannot be fitted into a scientific way of looking at things. Those who think that the only knowledge worth anything is scientific knowledge are quite apt to dismiss the Bible as irrelevant and untrue. It is against such a form of criticism that the biblical statement quoted above rightly protests.

But adverse criticism is not the only type of criticism or the only proper use of the word. A music critic, a drama critic, or a book reviewer who is asked to give a critique of a recent, important work is expected to be an expert in his field. He will not demonstrate his wisdom by passing only negative judgments. To do this on great productions would show not expert knowledge but simply a sour or cynical spirit that would soon disqualify him for his task. Instead, he must bring all the resources of his own knowledge to whatever he is criticizing, explore the deeper meanings that the general public might overlook, and pass as fair a judgment as possible. In short, he must be an interpreter rather than a fault-finder.

It is this kind of criticism in which most biblical scholars have been engaged in the past century. Because of their work we understand the Bible better and see deeper and richer meanings in it than would have been possible without their work. They have brought to the Bible linguistic, historical, and scientific knowledge. Furthermore, these scholars have usually been persons of deep faith whose love for God and for the Bible have led them to their tasks. Their services, which have been of incalculable value in opening up the message of the Bible to a world that but dimly grasped it or that rejected it as archaic, should be deeply appreciated.

One type of such criticism has been called *textual,* because it aims to get back to the most authentic original form of the text, digging through the accretions and changes that came with copying and recopying. Since all of the Bible was written many centuries before printing was invented and because in no instance do we have the original as it was written first-hand by its author, the work of the textual critic is very important. It is closely related to the importance of the best possible translation. For example, the Revised Standard Version gives a great advantage in clarity and accuracy over the King James Version of 1611, though some persons still prefer the King James because of its familiarity and beauty.

A second type is *historical* (sometimes called *higher*)

criticism, which aims to provide a better understanding of the message of the Bible by viewing its different books from the standpoint of the period when they were written and the social setting, historical circumstances, and climate of thought in those times. With this is usually joined also a study of the kind of literary form that is used and of the purpose of the author. This is needed because the Bible is not one book but a library of sixty-six books. Not all of it is history, for it also contains poetry, philosophy, folklore, genealogy, law codes, sermons, letters, and much else that must be viewed in the light of what its authors in those times were trying to say through these varied literary forms. Such a study leads to what has been stated earlier in this chapter—that the Bible is not in every word an infallible revelation of God, but that it is a record made through human instruments of the way in which God was teaching, guiding, rebuking, sustaining, and ever seeking to redeem and save his people.

For example, the Bible was written in a pre-scientific age and was never intended to serve as a book of science. Accordingly, it is futile to try to find a scientific account of creation in the great prose poem with which the Book of Genesis opens. Yet this does not set aside the tremendous spiritual truth expressed in the words "In the beginning God created the heavens and the earth." Wrestle as we may with the problem of pain in God's world, there is still a meaning in the refrain of that story, "And God saw that it was good," which neither philosophy nor science can set aside.

Textual and historical criticism meet in a special kind of literary study called *form criticism*. Many of the books of the Bible, including the Synoptic Gospels—Matthew, Mark and Luke, from which much of our knowledge of the words and deeds of Jesus is derived—are compilations from earlier manuscripts and fragments. These were apparently put together following certain patterns; and form criticism, which is a highly technical study, attempts to sort these out. At the beginning of this kind of study some feared that our faith in Jesus might be challenged. On the contrary, however, we understand him better than before.

In recent years there have been important archeological discoveries in Palestine. The discovery of the Dead Sea Scrolls in 1947 and later has been an event of the first magnitude. On the whole they corroborate rather than contradict the history given in the Bible. But more important than historical accuracy is the way in which the timeless and eternal spiritual truths of the Bible speak to us today.

The Bible gives us a world with God in it, through it, and above it. It gives us Christ to show us God and teach us the way of love. It gives us the Spirit of God in the living Christ ever near to bless, to comfort, and to strengthen us. It shows us how we ought to live during our years on earth and promises us an eternal home with God. It offers forgiveness of sin and victory over pain, sin, and death. It is therefore the most important book in the world. It is contemporary because it is timeless. When we read the Bible not merely with credulous but with receptive minds and hearts, God speaks to us through it. Indeed, "it is God's eternal Word to every generation."

5

We Believe in Man

*W*E HOLD *as central the dignity and sacredness of every human personality. Man is made in the spiritual image of God and partakes of His character and fellowship. He is greater than the world through which God produces and sustains His life. The Scriptures remind us that man is a sinner and has fallen short of the glory of God. He may, however, through grace, rise above his sin and the circumstances which surround him. His glory is in his humanity and not his race or color. Endowed with freedom of choice, he may descend to the lowest hell or rise to the highest heaven. In him as a person all the moral ends of the universe and all the movement of God's eternal purpose find meaning and value.*

WHAT IS MAN?

Within recent years the psalmist's question,

"What is man that thou art mindful of him,
and the son of man that thou dost care for him?" [12]

has swung into a central place of interest in both theological and popular thinking. A generation ago the existence and nature of God and his relation, if any, to what seems to be a cruel and morally indifferent universe, occupied many

[12] Psalms 8:4.

minds. This interest has not ceased, as previous chapters have indicated. But the dominant questions today appear to be "Who am I? What am I? What am I here for? Where am I going?" Many differences of opinion—important to the individual and crucial to society—center in the answers to these questions.

Ever since the publication of Reinhold Niebuhr's now classic two volumes of the Gifford Lectures, *The Nature and Destiny of Man*,[13] this theme has been dominant in theological circles. Even if Niebuhr had not written these books, the subject was ripe for re-examination, for formerly prevalent optimistic views of man's powers were waning both from the pressure of events and from the shift in theology from philosophical to biblical foundations. Karl Barth, Emil Brunner, and the rediscovery of Sören Kierkegaard had great influence. Furthermore, European theology in general laid great stress on man's sin and his inability to save himself even by his best and noblest works.

The differences between liberalism and the new orthodoxy center more in the doctrine of man than at any other point. The former stresses man's dignity and greatness as the child of God made in the divine image while the latter stresses man's perpetual sinfulness and weakness. There is not an absolute difference between the two, for both admit the truth in the other's position. The emphasis in each is different, however. And, as we shall see in the next chapter, this makes a difference as to how we will regard a subject of major importance—man's salvation.

In popular circles the focus of questioning has shifted from God to man. This does not mean that man has recently become more important than God, for men always tend to put themselves in the center even when they claim to exalt God above all. Yet people seem to be less worried about God and more concerned about themselves than they were a generation ago. God may generally be taken for granted.

[13] New York: Charles Scribner's Sons, Volume I, 1941; Volume II, 1943.

The matters of real concern are our inner tensions and, on the other side of the ledger, our sources of satisfaction. The demands constantly being made upon us in business and family life, the world scene, and the precarious state in which we all dwell compel thoughtful people to consider the nature and destiny of man. Although salvation—if labeled in religious terminology—can hardly be called one of man's dominant interests, modes of escape from ourselves and our boredom and insecurities are much desired and talked about by the general public. The vogue of psychiatry and of various "peace of mind" cults—whether overtly religious or not— give evidence that modern man is gravely concerned about himself.

What, then, does our Christian faith tell us not only about modern man but about man in every age?

MAN IN THE DIVINE IMAGE

We hold as central the dignity and sacredness of every human personality. Man is made in the spiritual image of God and partakes of His character and fellowship.

We referred in the previous chapter to the great beauty, dignity, and spiritual truths to be found in the first chapter of Genesis. One of its greatest verses is Genesis 1:27 which says, "So God created man in his own image, in the image of God he created him; male and female he created them."

Obviously this cannot mean that man looks like God in the sense that a child may have the color of eyes or the facial contour of a parent. It means something far deeper. It means that in our basic nature—our essential nature, if one prefers that term—God has made us as much like himself as a finite creature can be like the Infinite. God is all wise, wholly righteous, altogether loving, and supreme in creative power. Our wisdom, goodness, love, and creativity are limited. They are never infinite and are often very feeble, especially when we fail to make use of our God-given powers.

Yet these are great gifts—gifts of immeasurable importance in our estimate of the worth of human personality.

What it means to be made in the image of God may become clearer if we take a look at our most distinctive traits —those that set us apart from the sub-human world and prompt us to speak of "the human soul" or "the human spirit."

There is, first, God's great gift of *freedom of choice and decision*. This gift is never unlimited; it is often misused; yet it is always present to distinguish man from anything else in all creation. We are not mere biological organisms acting by instinct or reflexes; we are free within limits to direct our destinies by ideals and goals. From this power comes man's *capacity for goodness* which, with the alternative possibility of evil, places on us a great responsibility. With it also comes our *capacity for learning*—the possibility of acquiring the great heritage of the past, of seeking and discovering truth, and of using our powers for fresh forms of creativity. Immensely important though this privilege is, God has bestowed an even greater gift, the *capacity for loving*. On this is built all human fellowship. It is a capacity that is far more than biological instinct or animal gregariousness. Because we have it, we are bidden to love God supremely and our neighbors as ourselves.

Reference was made above to our *creativity*. Since we receive this gift from God, the Creator of all, he calls us to serve him and one another in fashioning more nearly to his purposes an unfinished world. And because of our *evaluating* powers, we can discern between the higher and the lower, set standards and goals to work toward, and by God's help —if we are faithful stewards of his gifts—can succeed in some measure in making the world around us better. These are some of the things that give man a high dignity and which provide meaning to the thought of our being made in God's image.

Because God has loved and trusted us enough to make us

in his image, we ought never to think meanly or to speak disparingly of any human being, including ourselves. This does not mean that we ought to have no humility, for we have plenty of sins and weaknesses to keep us humble! Yet the major note in our doctrine of man may well be man's essential greatness—greatness not of our own achieving but as God's gift. Taken seriously, this is a tremendous challenge both to live worthily and to treat all other persons with great dignity and respect.

Another idea in the thought of the divine image which we ought not to miss is suggested in the last words of the sentences quoted above. God made us in his own image *for fellowship with himself*. This is the highest tribute he could pay us. Certainly we need the lift and the deepening of spirit which come from fellowship with God. But may it not also be that God, the Infinite and the Eternal, needs our fellowship for the completion of *his* experience? If so, let us not grieve him by denying him this. We must examine the meaning of this idea in a later chapter on Christian experience.

MAN AS NATURE AND SPIRIT

He is greater than the world through which God produces and sustains his life. . . . Endowed with freedom of choice, he may descend to the lowest hell or rise to the highest heaven.

The Bible does not ordinarily split man's personality into body and soul or make the three-pronged division of body, mind, and soul which we are inclined to make. Man (*adham* in the Hebrew, from whence comes "Adam" as generic man) is one person. He lives as a whole; he dies as a whole; he is resurrected as a whole. Yet this does not mean that the Bible simply identifies man with his body and its behavior, as the behavioristic or other naturalistic psychologists are inclined to do. Man is "like the beasts that perish"

(Psalms 49:12, 20) in his mortality, but not in his honor. And where the biblical writers felt the need to distinguish between the body's needs and impulses and those of the soul, they did not hesitate to do so.[14] Paul, who makes the contrast more often than does any other writer, is very clear that the body is good in itself—so good that it is a temple of the Holy Spirit. Regardless of this fact, however, he realizes that it has impulses that must ever be kept in subordination to the soul.

The true relation of man to the physical world—including that part of it which is his own body—is that through nature "God produces and sustains his life." If we follow the example of Jesus, we shall find nothing small or insignificant in all God's world. Yet man is God's supreme creation, greater than anything else in all existence. To cite again the Genesis story, God has given man the right to "have dominion," that is, to exercise stewardship, over all that he has made (Genesis 1:28-29). Taken seriously, this could transform our economic life and help the modern world recover the Protestant Reformation's sense of the sacredness of the common life of daily labor. To cite from another angle, the late Archbishop William Temple's phrase, this is a "sacramental universe" in which all nature speaks of God, its Creator. Furthermore, Temple concludes, Christianity is the most "materialistic" of all religions because, though it subordinates matter to spirit, it finds sacredness in everything God has made.[15]

We have noted that God has made man the steward of his world and has given him great responsibilities. God has also given man freedom of choice in which moral responsibility is centered. Because of this freedom he can worship and serve God and give himself in great devotion to what is involved in the Christian life. But because of the misuse of this freedom, every man sins. This is man's perennial plight, and in

[14] Note, for example, Matthew 10:28; Luke 12:4; 1 Corinthians 6:13-20; 9:27.
[15] *Nature, Man and God* (New York: St. Martin's Press, Inc.) pp. 473-495.

the deeper issues of his being he cannot save himself. Having seen realistically that this is true, let us look further at what it means.

MAN AS SINNER

The Scriptures remind us that man is a sinner and has fallen short of the glory of God. He may, however, through grace, rise above his sin and the circumstances which surround him.

Indeed, the Scriptures remind us that man is a sinner! This fact is written on every page of the Bible, and the Bible's great theme is God's loving concern for his sinning people and his gracious forgiveness of those who in penitence will turn to him for newness of life.

But the Bible is not so explicit concerning what sin is. Sometimes it is conceived *legalistically*, as disobedience to the Ten Commandments or to some other code of law. The Pharisees of Jesus' time had a very elaborate and definite set of rules listing things that could not be done without falling into sin. These restrictions were particularly rigid in regard to the Sabbath. Jesus felt obligated to rebuke such legalism. To him it was sinful to "tithe mint and dill and cummin," when neglecting "the weightier matters of the law, justice and mercy and faith." (Matthew 23:23.) He predicted condemnation for men who like to "go about in long robes, and to have salutations in the market places and the best seats in the synagogues and the places of honor at feasts, who devour widows' houses and for a pretense make long prayers." (Mark 12:38-40.)

Such legalistic views of righteousness, and correspondingly, of sin, have their counterparts today. But more common is the *moralistic* idea of sin. This idea pictures sin in terms of infractions of prevailing moral and social standards. In short, to sin is to do "what isn't done," whether this means getting drunk, having an illegitimate baby, robbing a bank, or committing a murder. To object to such a standard is not to say that these things are right; clearly they are not. Yet human standards, which vary from age to age and from place to place, are not enough. To sin is something far more serious than to break either the written or unwritten laws of society, for all sin in its real meaning is sin against God.

The Bible declares again and again that the deeper meaning of sin is *disobedience to God*. Such disobedience may or may not lead us into courses of action that society condemns. The prophets have always proclaimed a higher morality than their surrounding cultures. This is why Jesus was crucified and why his followers have again and again been misunderstood and persecuted. Yet all of these have suffered victoriously because they knew that fidelity to God was all that really mattered.

Sin means disobedience, and guilt before God is the only ultimate form of guilt. But this does not mean that how we treat our brothers is irrelevant! It matters enormously, for according to Jesus the highest goodness consists in love to God which obligates us also to love our neighbor. And because Jesus has thus made love the supreme demand of the New Testament faith, lovelessness is the corresponding evil.

The forms in which we manifest our lack of love are manifold. Sometimes we express it in acute forms of hatred and in positive and terrible acts of injury. Again—probably more often and certainly more insidiously—it appears in callous indifference, coldness of heart, and moral dullness to the needs and feelings of others. Yet whatever the form, we sin whenever we fail to love. This is man's perennial tendency, and it is so deep-seated that only God can purge and transform our living. About this we shall be doing some more thinking in the next chapter. But let us conclude this discussion with a further look at the difference the Christian understanding of man makes in our human, social situation.

MAN AND HIS WORLD

*His glory is in his humanity and not his race or color.
. . . In him as a person all the moral ends of the universe
and all the movement of God's eternal purpose find meaning
and value.*

If what has been said thus far is true, all of us—despite
our sinfulness—are infinitely precious and worthwhile to
God. This is true regardless of our human estimates and our
social situation. We may be white or colored; Caucasian,
Semitic, or Mongolian; American, European, or Oriental;
tall or short; rich or poor; educated or illiterate; male or
female—God loves and prizes us all. The only true and vital
ground of democracy lies in this fact. It is only as this fact
is more fully recognized and wrought into our living that we
shall have any semblance of human justice in our society.

It should be apparent without any lengthy argument that
race discrimination, any assumptions of class superiority,
or cleavages based on a self-righteous pride of national
origin must be utterly abhorrent to God. This is not to say
that race or national differences are wrong in themselves.
Just as there is no moral quality in the fact that persons are
born male or female, so these other human differences are
facts. What is terribly wrong is to make of them tools of
dominance of one group over another and to erect walls of
division among persons. Our common humanity ought to be
the basis of equality and fellowship.

But can we agree on the last statement of the quoted
paragraph regarding man—the idea that "in him as a person
all the moral ends of the universe and all the movement of
God's eternal purpose find meaning"? This is a large statement, and some persons might find it presumptuous!
Whether it *is* presumptuous depends wholly on the ground
on which it is made. If man is simply trying to exalt himself and is seeking to claim for himself the central spotlight
of the universe, then it is worse than presumptuous; it is

blasphemous. But if the Christian in all humility subordinates himself to God and recognizes his sin and weakness and his complete dependence on God for his existence and his salvation, there is nothing wrong in thinking that man is the supreme object of God's concern. Jesus apparently believed this, and so may we.

Jesus believed in man's great value to God enough to live and to die for our redemption. To this great theme let us now turn.

6

We Believe in Salvation FromSin

THIS experience comes through faith in Jesus Christ as Saviour and Lord. The act involves penitence for past sins and the acceptance of His mercy and forgiveness. Salvation comes not by our own striving or any achievement of merit. It is the free gift of God's grace who "shows his love for us in that while we were yet sinners Christ died for us." Thus God takes away our sins, restores His image in our hearts, and grants to us a new birth, another chance, through the unmerited love of His Son and our Saviour, Jesus Christ.

DO WE NEED SALVATION?

In the third chapter of John's Gospel we read of a man named Nicodemus, a Pharisee and a ruler of the Jews, who came to Jesus by night with a searching and uneasy sense that Jesus could give him something that he needed greatly. Jesus' words to him on that occasion are as challenging today as they were in the first century: "Truly, truly, I say to you, unless one is born anew, he cannot see the kingdom of God." (John 3:3.)

Nicodemus did not understand what it could mean to be "born anew," and many persons since his time have failed to understand. But those who became Christians in the first century knew. Their lives were set aflame by a new spirit that took them through "dungeon, fire, and sword," and in this experience the Church was born. The new birth has lain at the heart of the gospel ever since.

But do we need salvation today? How does a saved person differ from a decently moral, well-behaved, public-spirited citizen who is not a Christian? And do we need any special experience in order to become a Christian? These questions may be hard to answer, but they ought to be faced.

It is both the blessing and the curse of our society that there are so many "good" people who are not Christians. It is a blessing in that we are happy about their kindness, generosity, and self-control. But it is a curse in that when a person is a fairly good citizen and a decent fellow, he is likely to assume he is good enough. In this case "the good is the enemy of the best."

This is no new phenomenon. The rich ruler who came to Jesus with the searching question "Good teacher, what shall I do to inherit eternal life?" had kept the commandments from his youth. But this was not enough. (Luke 18:18-23.) Although the Bible does not say so, Nicodemus could probably have made a similar claim.

To the situation as it exists today, several conclusions can be drawn:

1. We ought not to decry real goodness or lambaste it as evil. Instead, we should rejoice in it wherever it is found.

2. We ought not to suppose that being a kind neighbor or having a "well-adjusted personality" is a true equivalent for life in the Kingdom.

3. We must start with people where they are—whether serene and kindly or tragically upset and maladjusted— if we are to be God's servants to bring them to Christian salvation.

The answer to this problem roots in what we must be saved *from* if we are to be saved by Christ. Traditionally, the emphasis has been placed almost entirely on being saved from sin. Since this is man's most persistent enemy, it is certainly our basic need. Even in our free-and-easy generation hosts of people are tortured with the agony of remorse. And more, perhaps, would be if dullness had not seared their consciences.

However, there is another need to which Jesus was always ministering, and another situation in which regeneration (the historic phrase for being "born anew") has been the gift of God through Christ in all the centuries. This is the need for peace of soul, for conquest of fear, for strength in weakness, for the ability to "be of good cheer" even in the face of deepest trouble, and to be "faithful unto death" where death is real and terrible and not to be evaded.

Today we recognize that not only sin but neuroses of various sorts are terribly disturbing to personalities. Our generation is no more sinful than any in the past, but it is more jittery. Many of our contemporaries to whom Christian regeneration seems quaintly out of date are inwardly crying out for exactly what it has given to Christians through many centuries: courage and inner peace.

Sometimes we call this condition "peace of mind" and either seek it or decry it, according to our inclinations. There is a superficial peace of mind that is not the same as Christian peace and is more of an escape than an acceptance of the hard realities of life. But there is also a peace that comes from God, "a peace that the world cannot give." It is this that we are concerned with here.

Therefore our message must always have two sides. On the one hand, we must uncover the sins of which most people are largely unconscious—the all-too-prevalent sins of pettiness, harshness, jealousy, self-pity, and self-will—and call men to repentance as the basic requirement of the new life in Christ. We must also with understanding and sympathy mediate to unhappy, anxious, turbulent lives the gift of the peace of God which passes all understanding.

But the question "Do we need salvation?" is a two-pronged

one. Although we realize that persons need what the Christian religion offers, must we insist that a person who has "grown up a Christian" still needs to have the experience of personal regeneration? Are not the influences of a Christian home and church enough to make him a Christian without his having to be "born again?"

Certainly not everybody must have the dramatic about-face experience of Paul on the Damascus road or an experience like that of Augustine, who was a seeker for years until, at thirty-two, he suddenly answered the call of Christ and became a changed man. But the experiences of Martin Luther and John Wesley are also significant. Both of these men had been Christians during their youth in a second-hand sort of way and were servants of the church. But they, too, lacked great vitality until a personal experience gripped and transformed their lives.

It is to say too much to claim that nobody can be a Christian on the basis of Christian nurture, but it is to say too little to underestimate the need of a personal decision for Christ. Such a decision may be overwhelming in its emotional effect and may change radically the currents of one's vocational, domestic, and community relations. Or it may be made quietly and may lead primarily to deepening rather than the discarding of previously formed ideals and goals. But there must be personal decision, or Christian experience remains marginal and inert.

About the nature of Christian experience we shall have more to say in the next chapter. Now we must turn to two other crucial questions: What does God do in our salvation? And what does he require of us?

JUSTIFICATION BY FAITH

This experience comes through faith in Jesus Christ as Saviour and Lord. The act involves penitence for past sins and the acceptance of His mercy and forgiveness. Salvation

*comes not by our own striving or any achievement of merit.
It is the free gift of God's grace who "shows his love for us
in that while we were yet sinners Christ died for us."*

The cardinal note of the Protestant Reformation, and one
that in some form has been a major emphasis of most Protestant denominations, is justification by faith. It was this emphasis that became life-transforming for Martin Luther. It
enabled him to break with the church of Rome and its ex-
ternal system of salvation, and under persecution to speak
these historic words at the Diet of Worms: "Here I stand;
I can do no other." Furthermore, it was Luther's com-
mentary on the Book of Romans, wherein this doctrine is
proclaimed, which was heard by John Wesley as he attended
the meeting on Aldersgate Street. And it was in this same
meeting that his heart was "strangely warmed" and Methodism was born.

What does this doctrine mean? In brief, it means that our
salvation is God's gift and not our achievement. It means
that what he requires of us are penitence, faith, and the acceptance of his mercy and forgiveness. Salvation does not
come "by our own striving or any achievement of merit." In
other words, we are not saved by our own good works, however good they may be. We are not saved by our own merits,
however meritorious our acts. We are saved by God's gift
in the ministry and death of Christ as we accept these gifts in
a humble and penitent spirit and dedicate our lives to God.

Some common misunderstandings concerning the doctrine
should also be cleared away. To be "justified" means that
God no longer holds us under judgment for our past sins.
Instead, he lifts the burden of our sinning and gives us a
new start. This gives a new power of moral victory to our
lives. As one of the great hymns by Charles Wesley puts it:

> "He breaks the power of canceled sin,
>   He sets the prisoner free." [16]

[16] From "O For a Thousand Tongues to Sing."

Yet this does not mean that our sins, either past, present, or future, are a matter of indifference to God. Sin, whether forgiven or unforgiven, is always a serious matter. Nor does it mean that the social and personal effects of past sins are all wiped out. Sin leaves its scars even where wounds are healed. The persons we have hurt through our selfishness and lack of love may forgive us, but this does not make the situation as if it had never happened. To be born anew is a wonderful and life-changing experience, transforming our relations to one another as well as to God. But it cannot set aside all the past, and we ought not to expect it to.

Nor does the experience of being justified by faith through the grace of God put an end to our sinning! There is a great wealth of meaning and truth in the words of Paul, "Therefore, since we are justified by faith, we have peace with God through our Lord Jesus Christ." (Romans 5:1.) And there is much wisdom in Paul's other message of assurance which is basic to the subject of this chapter: "Therefore, if any one is in Christ, he is a new creation; the old has passed away, behold, the new has come." (2 Corinthians 5:17.) This is what regeneration—being born anew—means. Conversion, which is the word we commonly use for this experience, stresses the turning from a self-centered to a God-centered life. Therefore it is the new orientation by which life is governed.

All this may be said and must be said. Yet the fact remains that we do not by conversion become sinless. We must repent again and again and daily seek God's forgiveness. As was noted earlier, there is great truth in the words of Luther, *simul justus et peccator,* which mean "at the same time justified and a sinner." This is the great paradox of our faith. It does not contradict the fact that we are called of God and enabled by him to "grow in grace." And, as we shall see in a later chapter, this is the basic meaning of Christian perfection and sanctification. It *does* contradict any doctrine of holiness which assumes that either through an initial regeneration or a "second blessing" we shall achieve on earth the ability to live without sin. To assume that we have reached this pinnacle, or shall reach it, is a dangerous pitfall to self-righteousness. We need at this point to keep ever before us the words of Paul, "Therefore let any one who thinks that he stands take heed lest he fall." (1 Corinthians 10:12.)

The Difference Salvation Makes

Thus God takes away our sins, restores His image in our hearts, and grants us a new birth, another chance, through the unmerited love of His Son and our Saviour, Jesus Christ.

Salvation means being delivered from the burden of our sins and the torturing pangs of remorse by the awareness that God has forgiven us and set before us the possibility of a new life. A psychological term much heard today is "acceptance." Salvation means that the love of God accepts us as we are and enables us, not indifferently or self-righteously, but humbly, penitently, and with new dedication of will, to accept ourselves. Another psychological term is 'integration." In the Christian sense our discordant, confused, sinful lives are given a new wholeness and sense of direction. To be saved means to be healed—made whole from our infirmity of soul and given a new strength and purpose from God.

There is no one word that expresses the full meaning of salvation. Yet all the great traditional words of our faith indicate a genuine change of life, goals, and motive power. As regeneration in its derivation means to be "born again," and as conversion means to "turn around," so redemption means to be "bought back" and brought back to our Father's home and fellowship through the love and the self-giving of Christ. Atonement means "at-one-ment" and refers to the new unity of the soul with God which one who has been alienated and estranged by his sin and self-will finds in the grace, mercy, and peace that God in Christ stands ready to impart. Reconciliation does not mean that God must be reconciled to us, but that "God was in Christ reconciling the world to himself, not counting their trespasses against them, and entrusting to us the message of reconciliation" (2 Corinthians 5:19). The story of the prodigal son is perhaps the greatest of all Jesus' parables because it expresses so perfectly what the love of God has done and is always doing for us.

Today we are perhaps more likely to use simply the words "accepting Christ" or "becoming a Christian" for this great event, but the meaning is the same. It means being "born again" in the center of one's being and hence having a new outlook and approach to life.

If the regeneration is deep-going, a person's choices and decisions are different from the time when it happens. Feelings, words, and acts take on a different tenor. "He seems like a new person" or "I feel like a new man" are commonplace but accurate descriptions of the change that can be wrought.

Sometimes the change is so radical that it seems miraculous. Sometimes there is a gradual, and at times almost imperceptible, change in values, motives, feelings, and modes of responding to situations. If there is no difference at all, regeneration has not occurred.

To be real, regeneration must certainly affect our moral living. This does not mean that a radical and drastic change in moral standards is always involved. Yet it must sharpen our sensitivity to the needs and hurts of others; it must increase our eagerness to serve; it must sharpen our courage under moral strain—or it is shallow. Though opinions may legitimately differ as to what is the right course to take in a given issue, especially in a complex matter, the saved Christian stands for the right as he sees it. The committed Christian is one about whom there is no doubt concerning which side he will be on in a clear-cut moral issue or how he will

meet a moral crisis that might shake another person from
his moorings.

Regeneration begins inevitably in personal experience. It
was not simply an accident that led Jesus to concentrate
on touching the inner lives of people and leading them to
trust and obey God in a new way. He knew, as we also must
know if we are at all discerning, that this is where motives
are established and activities are grounded. The world we
live in sadly needs reconstructing. But there can be no greatly reconstructed world until there are more reconstructed
persons in it. This means that even those who call themselves Christians must become more deeply Christian.

Yet this does not by any means give sanction to indifference to social issues. Jesus found his mission perfectly stated
in certain great words of the prophet Isaiah:

> "The Spirit of the Lord is upon me,
> because he has anointed me to preach good news
>   to the poor.
> He has sent me to proclaim release to the captives
> and recovering of sight to the blind,
> to set at liberty those who are oppressed,
> to proclaim the acceptable year of the Lord." [17]

At the call of Christ, this may well be our mission in our
own time and place. Is it an individual or social gospel? It is
both, and the two cannot be separated without distortion.

Accordingly, a regenerated Christian looks outward in
sympathy and service to other people—all people of all races,
classes, and nations. He takes so seriously the injunction to
love God and his neighbor that he cannot be at ease before injustice, evil-doing, or the suffering of others. The parable of
the Good Samaritan takes its place alongside that of the
Prodigal Son as being central to our faith.

"Truly, truly, I say to you, unless one is born anew, he

[17] Luke 4:18-19.

cannot see the kingdom of God." This is a large order. It is too great for both our comprehension and our power. But it is not too great for God, "who has shone in our hearts to give the light of the knowledge of the glory of God in the face of Jesus Christ." (2 Corinthians 4:6.)

7

We Believe in Christian Experience

*I*T IS *the privilege of every redeemed soul to know his sins are forgiven and to be assured, through the co-operating witness of the Holy Spirit with his spirit, that he is a child of God. Reason, like the Law, may be the schoolmaster leading us to Christ. Yet our deepest assurance is not the result of reason but of repentance and faith. Our faith is often and unashamedly suffused with intense feeling. Yet our assurance arises not out of emotion but out of the radiant certainty of an indwelling Christ, whose mercy has cleansed us, whose love has saved us, and whose presence within our hearts has given us power and victory. The experience of the whole man, evaluating Scripture, tradition, and reason, through the vital action of the Holy Spirit, becomes the ultimate authority in religious certainty.*

DO WE KNOW WE ARE SAVED?

In modern times people tend to recoil from the evangelism of an earlier day in which individuals were encouraged to accost others—sometimes even complete strangers—with the blunt question, "Are you saved?" Even modern forms of mass evangelism in which this same question is put very pointedly by the evangelist and great stress is laid upon the assurance of salvation are under suspicion by many.

72

The reasons for feeling this way are partly legitimate and partly not so justifiable. As the previous chapter has indicated, to experience Christian salvation is not a human achievement. It is the unmerited gift of God to the penitent sinner, and the mood of humble awareness of our own short-comings introduces an understandable reticence about claiming too much or announcing it too publicly. A person often feels that it is more appropriate to say modestly, "I am trying with God's help to be a Christian." Furthermore, to be a Christian is no "single-track" or simple matter to be settled by going forward or signing a card in an evangelistic meeting. It is not a matter that can be settled even by taking the public step of joining the church. Instead, it relates to the whole of life and its reorientation. Who, then, is bold enough —if he is thoroughly honest with himself—to affirm without any qualification:

> 'Tis done: the great transaction's done!
> I am my Lord's, and He is mine.[18]

Yet these considerations, which are legitimate and Christian, are not the whole story. It was in the mood of humble awareness of imperfection and lack of full achievement in Christian experience that Paul wrote, "Brethren, I do not consider that I have made it my own; but one thing I do, forgetting what lies behind and straining forward to what lies ahead, I press on toward the goal for the prize of the upward call of God in Christ Jesus." (Philippians 3:13-14.) Yet Paul had not the slightest doubt that God had wrought a great transformation in his life. The verse immediately preceding the one just quoted affirms this unequivocally with the reason for his pressing forward: "I press on to make

[18] From "O Happy Day That Fixed My Choice," by Philip Doddridge.

it my own, because Christ Jesus has made me his own."
(Philippians 3:12.) [19]

It is a paradox of our faith—but one that Christian living
validates—that we should feel assured of our salvation when
our lives have been committed to God in Christ; yet at
the same time we should "press on," in humility and continuing penitence, leaving it to God to judge our status before him. It is wrong to boast of being a Christian or to assume that all our moral struggle is over. It is right to feel
confident that a new power has come into our lives through
Christ, for which we give him all the glory and the praise of
a grateful heart.

How Do We Know?

*It is the privilege of every redeemed soul to know his sins
are forgiven and to be assured, through the co-operating witness of the Holy Spirit with his spirit, that he is a child of
God. Reason, like the Law, may be the schoolmaster leading
us to Christ. Yet our deepest assurance is not the result of
reason but of repentance and faith.*

This passage calls our attention to four grounds of assurance: the witness of the Holy Spirit, reason, repentance, and
faith. All four are needed, and each needs the others to
avoid distortion.

The Holy Spirit, as we saw in chapter 3, is God present
and God active within our lives. To say, then, that the Holy
Spirit gives assurance of salvation is to say that God himself
gives us this assurance. And against this there can be no
contention. The real question—and a very difficult one indeed—is whether *what we take to be* the voice of the Holy
Spirit is in reality the voice of God or is simply the up-

[19] The "it" in these verses refers specifically to "the resurrection from the
dead" (verse 11). Yet the whole context of the passage indicates that Paul is
not speaking primarily about the resurrection after death but to new life in the
present through knowing Christ as Savior.

cropping of our own self-centered impulses. People have been known to slander and slaughter each other and even in religious matters to display a self-righteousness that is more diabolical than godlike on the assumption that they were being directed by the voice of the Holy Spirit. What then?

This very crucial question has been discussed in chapter 3 and some suggestions are given there for helping us decide when the Spirit speaks. The most basic one is to remember that the Holy Spirit is the living Christ, and that we must bring all our feelings and impulses under the light of his judgment and his great assurances. It was in dealing with this matter or one closely related to it that Paul wrote, "For it is the God who said, 'Let light shine out of darkness,' who has shone in our hearts to give the light of the knowledge of the glory of God in the face of Christ." (2 Corinthians 4:6.)

The term "reason" is perhaps a surprising one to use in reference to our assurance of salvation. We do not reason ourselves into a conviction that God has forgiven our sins unless we are "rationalizing" our behavior! Yet in reference to Christian experience as a whole, reason has a large part to play. In deciding what we ought to do in the many daily decisions that make up life, we must always think ahead, look at the situation as clearly and wisely as possible, and take the decisive step. We do this in faith, for we can never wholly read the future. But to take it in faith without using our heads is to court disaster. To cite a common but very important example, consider what happens when persons rush into marriages without using their reason! And just as surely as there is need to think as clearly as possible concerning this crucial step, so the matter of becoming a Christian is "not to be entered into unadvisedly, but reverently, discreetly, and in the fear of God."

Yet marriages based wholly on reason and not on faith and love are far from ideal. Unless reason leads the persons involved on to faith and love, such marriages are doomed.

To carry the analogy into Christian experience, reason may be the schoolmaster leading us to Christ. But only in repentance, faith, and love of God is Christian experience firmly grounded. These are matters of feeling rather than reasoned demonstration. They come to a focus in our loyalty to Christ as we attempt to be his followers, and loyalty is a commitment of will which is based on deep feeling. This leads us accordingly to examine the rightful place of feeling in Christian experience.

FEELING IN CHRISTIAN EXPERIENCE

Our faith is often and unashamedly suffused with intense feeling. Yet our assurance arises not out of emotion but out of the radiant certainty of an indwelling Christ, whose mercy has cleansed us, whose love has saved us, and whose presence within our hearts has given us power and victory.

It is out of feeling that the motive power of life is generated. Reason can sometimes settle for us what we ought to do, but only feeling can make us do it. This feeling may take the positive form of desire, interest, gratitude, or love. It may take the negative form of apprehension and the compulsion of "I must do this, or else. . . ." Often it takes the form of duty, which may be gladly accepted or done from a feeling of stern necessity. These feelings can become so firmly established that they are habitual and we no longer feel either an emotional glow or a great struggle within us. Yet the feeling is there, directing the currents of the subconscious. To cite the famous analogy of William James, which has been reinforced since his time by much more knowledge of depth psychology than was then available, personality is like an iceberg of which about one tenth is visible while the rest lies beneath the surface. It is in these great subconscious areas, more than of the surface, that feeling plays the dominant role in our behavior and living.

Yet often we are rightfully aware of intense feeling. If

these are positive emotions directed toward right persons, causes, or goals of action, we ought not to be ashamed of them or try to stifle them. Probably no one can generate an emotion simply by deciding that he would like to have it. Indeed this fact is at the root of the common affirmation that love cannot be commanded. But we can choose either to give free reign to an emotion or to suppress it. There are some emotions such as hate and envy which ought to be suppressed. Others, like the love, joy, and peace of which Paul speaks and which he calls the "fruit of the Spirit," ought to be gratefully accepted and fittingly expressed.

So we come again to the question of what feelings God desires us to have in Christian experience. Not the mere *force* of emotion but its *quality* is the true test of our Christian experience. And here we are led again to Christ as our standard. It is not because we feel a great emotional glow or a tremendous lift of spirit under eloquent preaching that makes us sure of salvation. These may be the temporary product of crowd psychology or may be similar to the emotions a person experiences when he gets carried away by the cheering around him at a ball game. Rather, the ground of our real transformation and the assurance of it is "the radiant certainty of an indwelling Christ, whose mercy has cleansed us, whose love has saved us, and whose presence within our hearts has given us power and victory."

Two questions then emerge. How shall we be witnesses to this saving, transforming, and strengthening faith in Christ? How shall we keep it among the daily demands of living? Both are very large questions on which there is space to say little, but the direction the answers take may be briefly suggested.

Christian experience normally emerges and is nourished within a fellowship—the fellowship of the church. It is important, therefore, for individuals to be connected with the worship, the sustaining companionship, and the service of the church if they are to become mature Christians.

Asking a person to join the church is not the same thing as asking him to become a Christian. But it may be the natural and necessary step he needs to take toward a personal decision for Christ. Increase in church membership is therefore closely related to evangelism, although it ought never to be supposed that the two are identical.

From the first century onward, Christian experience has been spread by means of personal witness and testimony. It is by telling the "good news" that the gospel is spread. And in this process, the spoken word—whether from pulpits or in a personal conversation—has had a large place. But it has never had the only place, and perhaps not the largest. How Christians have lived, whether in going to the lions under Nero's sadistic mania or in being Christian in the ordinary events of ordinary living, has been an indisputable witness.

Both laymen and ministers have a great opportunity and obligation to provide such a witness. As a person expresses his convictions in the activities of the church, in the family, in business, and in every kind of personal relations, he demonstrates beyond doubt what the Lord has done for him. Sometimes he demonstrates this in words, but always he shows it in acts and attitudes. Unless he expresses his Christian life by the kind of man he is, the world has legitimate reason to doubt whether the experience has either reality or depth.

Gaining a faith that is deep and real is no easy matter. If one is to succeed even partially, he must find a power greater than his own. In short, Christian experience must be nourished in prayer. This means both public worship and private prayer. Worship in church is familiar enough, but do we know how to pray?

For adult Christians most prayers learned in childhood do not express mature religious experience. The Lord's Prayer is an exception, but mechanical repetition and its very familiarity dull its force. The pulpit prayers one hears on Sunday are in behalf of a congregation and often sound unreal when transferred to one's private devotions. Printed prayers, however devout or beautiful, seldom seem quite personal enough. Because of these difficulties and also the pressures, strains, and competing interests of modern existence, many persons rarely pray.

There is no blueprint by which we can tell another person how to pray. There is no substitute for experience. The only way to learn to pray vitally is to resolve to pray and then keep at it. Yet we shall do better if we are clear concerning our aims.

"Prayer," as *The Westminster Shorter Catechism* puts it in matchless simplicity, "is an offering up of our desires unto God, for things agreeable to his will. . . ." [20] It is the attempt to become consciously aware of God's presence, to discover his will for our lives, to surrender our vagrant thoughts and self-centered desires to his controlling purpose, and to find in him power for living.

Although prayer may—and usually does—involve words, meditation, emotion, and action, it is no one of these by itself. Repetition of words—even great words like those of the Lord's Prayer—is mere muscular exercise, and our Lord himself warned against supposing that we could be heard for our much speaking. There are plenty of high thoughts that are not thoughts of the Most High. There are other good feelings which are not the lifting, life-changing feeling of the consciousness of God's presence. Prayer involves effort and should always bear fruit in action. But prayer itself centers in relaxed quietness—in the interruption of our own feverish activity that God may have a chance to act in us. From the human side, not *to do* but *to become* is its primary object.

Prayer has its human side, and its effects in us are not to be discounted. In reacting from the too simple idea that with sufficient faith prayer can change *anything,* we rightly emphasize the new power that we receive from it. But this, too, needs correction, for it is a mistake to suppose that the

[20] Question 98.

effectiveness of our praying depends mainly on what happens in *us*. We need the corrective of the psalmist who said, "I have set the Lord always before me." What happens in us is incidental to our praise and thanksgiving to God, our confession to God, the bringing of our desires before God, the commitment to God of our loved ones and of all we hold most dear. If God is the center of our praying, we do not need to worry about its effects in us. No prayer is ever futile which "sets the Lord before us."

THE EXPERIENCE OF THE WHOLE MAN

The experience of the whole man, evaluating Scripture, tradition, and reason, through the vital action of the Holy Spirit, becomes the ultimate authority in religious certainty.

This brings us to the final section in this chapter, which, in view of all that has been said, will not require many words.

Christian experience in depth and fullness can never be fragmentary. It is not to transformation or renewal in this or that aspect of our being that God calls us to accept salvation through Christ. It is to new faith, new loves, new joys, and new moral directions for the whole personality that he summons us. This does not mean we shall not have to work harder on some temptations than on others; we doubtless shall. But it is life as a whole, not life here or there, that is involved. "Therefore, if any one is in Christ, he is a new creation; the old has passed away, behold, the new has come." (2 Corinthians 5:17.)

Parallel with this great fact concerning the wholeness of Christian experience in its essential nature is our approach to it and our certainty of it. We do not know God in Christ through one channel only; we know him through the Bible, through the great Christian heritage of the Church, and through the best possible use of our minds. Our experiences in all of these areas are made real, personal, and vital through the Holy Spirit. One channel taken by itself may be deceptive.

We have seen that we can even misunderstand the Holy Spirit. Taken together, our knowledge of God gained from all these sources is all the certainty we need. In this assurance we may serve God and rest in his peace.

But we must serve God as we must rest in him, or our Christian experience is fleeting. But can we do this? If so, how perfectly can we? We shall turn to a discussion of these questions in the next chapter.

8

We Believe in Christian Perfection

*G*OD'S *grace is manifested not only in the forgiveness of our sins but is also creatively redemptive, the power that works in us to make us
perfect in love. Nothing short of perfection, Christlikeness in thought, word, and deed, can measure
God's loving purpose for us. It is our faith that the
fundamental change wrought in the individual by
regeneration is a dynamic process which by growth
in grace moves toward "mature manhood, to the
measure of the stature of the fullness of Christ." We
may quench the Spirit and fall from grace but our
divine destiny is perfect love and holiness in this
life.*

Do We Believe in Christian Perfection?

Probably not all readers will agree with what the author
writes in this chapter, for the whole matter of Christian perfection is very much disputed. As will soon be evident, the
writer believes that Christian perfection—or holiness, as the
doctrine is more popularly called—stands in one sense for a
very important and vital truth. Understood in another sense,
it can be a false and even dangerous doctrine.

Numerous sects today—sometimes called holiness groups
and sometimes Pentecostal, although the two terms are not
exactly synonymous—make much of the experience called
"entire sanctification." As usually understood, this idea as-

sumes that God so completely cleanses persons of sin that they afterwards live in perfect holiness. When the term "Pentecostal" is used, it connotes an emphasis on an emotional experience of salvation akin to the coming of the Holy Spirit at Pentecost, after which this state of holiness is achieved or given. Usually these groups are conservative or fundamentalist in their theology, with a rather rigid set of doctrines based on a literal interpretation of the Bible. Because the New Testament speaks of Christ's return in visible form, the same groups quite often expect this Second Coming in the near future and hence are called adventist or premillennialist. Although there is a fairly common pattern that unites these various views, we are concerned in this chapter only with the doctrine of holiness or sanctification.

Within these groups are deeply committed Christians with a missionary outreach that prompts them to carry the gospel to many lands. If we travel in the Orient today, we can find them everywhere. We cannot, therefore, cast sneering glances in their direction. But we may admire their zeal and still believe them to be more wrong in their beliefs and less sinless in their living than they think themselves to be.

The basic flaw in this understanding of holiness is that it encourages self-deception and a dangerous self-righteousness. It encourages also a sense of superiority at variance with Christian humility, for a man can hardly think himself sinless and others sinful without this attitude. And because he wants to keep himself "unspotted from the world," he sometimes places strong emphasis on such "sins" as wearing lipstick, playing cards, or engaging in other worldly pursuits. Separateness to preserve the purity of belief and practice is thus encouraged rather than co-operation with other Christians for the service of the world. Usually not much fellowship exists either in organization or in personal relations between members of these groups and those in other churches. Sometimes this spirit breaks out in open attacks.

So, if we are to believe in Christian perfection, we must do so on another basis. Let us now see whether or not this is possible.

THE GOALS WE SEEK

God's grace is manifested not only in the forgiveness of our sins but is also creatively redemptive, the power that works in us to make us perfect in love. Nothing short of perfection, Christlikeness in thought, word, and deed, can measure God's loving purpose for us.

What this statement affirms was said long ago by the author of the Epistle to the Ephesians who wrote, "Speaking the truth in love, we are to grow up in every way into him who is the head, into Christ." (Ephesians 4:15.) "God's loving purpose for us," the goal that by God's help we keep pressing toward, is set by Christ, not by the standards of people around us or by our own ideas of what being a successful Christian entails. In short, our deepest desire must be for "Christlikeness in thought, word, and deed."

This is no small matter. It means walking in the way of the cross, being willing to suffer for others, and being true to the call of God even to the uttermost. It means being sensitive to the needs, hurts, and feelings of others and caring enough to speak the loving word and do the loving deed. It means thinking no evil in a censorious spirit of anyone, for while some acts and attitudes must be judged sinful, it was Christ's way to love the sinner even while condemning the sin. It means absolute integrity in all our dealings. It means concern, not only for those near us but for all God's children—our brothers of every race and nation, of every part of the world, and of every station in life. It means concern for those of the unborn future as well as for all persons in the present. Christlikeness in thought, word, and deed means taking our Christian experience and our Christian moral standards into the church, into politics and economics, and into family and community relations. It claims the whole of life.

In short, to be Christlike means to be completely unselfish and completely faithful in our obedience to the call of God. Can anyone say, in full honesty, that he has attained it? Most of us know persons who have attained this goal to a very high degree, and we rightly call them saints. Yet not one of these pure souls, whose true living is a radiant witness to the power of God in Christian redemption, would think of calling himself perfect. Call him a saint and he will protest, for in his Christian humility and knowledge of himself he knows very well how far short he falls of perfect Christlikeness and holiness.

Someone may say, "Perfect living is indeed impossible for any but our Lord himself. But what Christian perfection means is to be 'perfect in love,' that is, perfect in intention and attitude." John Wesley apparently believed in this possibility, although he never carried it to the extremes to which some of his followers have taken it.

Is such a goal really possible? It probably is possible, by the grace of God, to reach a point where we have no conscious awareness of anything but love for God and our fellowmen. If this is not mere hypocrisy or self-righteousness—and it need not be—it indicates that we have reached the point at which Christian attitudes have become the prevailing pattern of our lives. They have become habitual in the sense that there need not be a tremendous struggle every time an issue presents itself. This is as it should be, although the higher we go in this advance toward Christlikeness the less likely we shall be to boast about it.

But note that we said, "no conscious awareness of anything but love." What of our unconsciousness? Depth psychology has shown what Christians have long known intuitively: that the impulses of sin and selfishness go much deeper than the conscious mind. They gnaw and tear at the defenses of even the best of us. Relatively few sins are committed with the conscious awareness of wrong-doing, for persons have an almost unlimited capacity for rationalizing their impulses until they feel that while something might be wrong for other persons or under other circumstances, it is right *for them at that time*. The smitings of conscience, if any, come afterward.

And what of our sins of omission through unconcern or self-centeredness? Do we ever do enough for God and our neighbors? Granted that we might get to the point of committing no positive sin, what of the vast range of things we ought to do but have not done? We are driven back to the words of Paul, "None is righteous, no, not one." (Romans 3:10.)

Yet this failure in attainment by no means invalidates our goals. When Jesus said in the Sermon on the Mount, "You, therefore, must be perfect, as your heavenly Father is perfect" (Matthew 5:48), he said "You *must* be," not "You *shall* be." There is an imperative that drives us onward, even as there is a Power that works within us toward this goal. Although we may realize—and in the present writer's judgment we *must* realize—that we shall never be perfect either in deeds or in attitudes on earth, this fact does not nullify the really great achievements that we see in others. Nor does it exempt us from making the effort. There is still a divine imperative that beckons us forward, and the Holy Spirit goes with us to sanctify our living toward what ought to be an ever increasing holiness.

Growth in Grace

It is our faith that the fundamental change wrought in the individual by regeneration is a dynamic process which by growth in grace moves toward "mature manhood, to the measure of the structure of the fullness of Christ." We may quench the Spirit and fall from grace but our divine destiny is perfect love and holiness in this life.

This affirmation is in considerable measure a restatement of what preceded it. Yet it contains both a positive and a negative note of much importance.

The positive note is the dynamic character of Christian experience. To be a Christian is always a matter of becoming; it is not a problem of static being. After we take the first great step—whether under the emotional surge of a great revival meeting or in a quieter mood—we may feel that we are now "in" and wholly different. But does not disillusionment sometimes follow? There may indeed be one great decisive step which changes the orientation of one's life and, in looking backward, we see it standing out, luminous and clear above all others. It is normal and right that there should be a time of specific decision for Christ, even among those who have been nurtured in a Christian family and church from babyhood. A second-hand experience is never enough, for we do not simply drift into a personal relationship to Christ. Yet this decisive step, which may or may not have a great emotional accompaniment and which may come with dramatic suddenness or by a succession of gradual steps, is never the end of the road. To say we have arrived indicates that we have not really started.

This idea needs to be stressed, for to many people "being saved" means simply being sure of heaven. So fixed is this idea in many minds that it is often difficult to get a discussion of salvation on any other basis. Evangelistic preaching not infrequently centers in "getting right with God" before death overtakes us. Death is a serious matter, and that salvation through Christ must have in it the vista of eternity is basic in Christian faith. But to think of it solely, or even primarily, as salvation *from* hell and *to* heaven is to distort the emphasis that Jesus gave it throughout his ministry and teaching. He assured his followers of the certainty of life beyond the grave through the Father's love, and he had some stern and sobering words to say about divine judgment. Yet the major part of his teaching was directed to the obligations and opportunities of this life rather than the next. Not only the Sermon on the Mount but most of his parables have to do with how we ought to live in the present in responsive obedience to the Father's will. Essentially what is required of us is God-centered living based on faith and love.

If this is true, we cannot expect all at once to acquire maturity in faith and love. Such maturity, as in all other aspects of human growth, takes time, nurture, practice, and discipline. Accordingly, we ought not to expect a new Christian to have all the maturity of one who has behind him years of Christian living and praying and serving. Paul saw this clearly and spoke of the Corinthian Christians as "babes in Christ" whom he had fed "with milk, not solid food." (1 Corinthians 3:1, 2.) Yet he could also say in his great hymn of love written to these same Christians, "When I became a man, I gave up childish ways." (1 Corinthians 13:11.) So should it be with all of us, and for this growth God provides both the power and the pattern in Jesus Christ.

Whether or not we shall ever come to "perfect love and holiness in this life" is a question on which many Christians differ. Yet there is no question at all that we are bidden and enabled to grow toward "mature manhood, to the measure of the stature of the fullness of Christ." The injunction that stands as the closing words of Second Peter is basic to the need for and the possibility of growth in Christian holiness: "But grow in the grace and knowledge of our Lord and Savior Jesus Christ. To him be the glory both now and to the day of eternity. Amen."

The possibility, like the obligation, to grow in grace is positive and good. It gives meaning and zest to the Christian life. But what of the other side? Another possibility—and a peril that must be taken more seriously—is stated in the words "We may quench the Spirit and fall from grace."

There have been Christians whose implicit if not avowed assumption is "once in, always in." This has even been held by some great theologians, of whom John Calvin is the most noted exponent, as the doctrine of "irresistible grace." Persons who have held this view have done so on the basis of God's complete sovereignty in salvation. They insist that he elects persons who are to be saved and that he does not thereafter change his mind. Although such a doctrine is not very widely held any more, its effects remain.

Two things must be said unequivocally: first, that it is God who saves us and not we ourselves; and second, that God saves only those who in penitence and obedience respond to his proffered grace. If we do not so respond, we fail to meet the conditions he lays upon us and thus we cannot lay claim to salvation.

If this failure to respond to him is true in regard to the decisive step of accepting Christ as our Lord and Savior, it is equally true of every step along the way. God never ceases to love us; his Holy Spirit never ceases to seek us out. Yet our indifference and unrepentant continuance in sin may "quench the Spirit" in our lives. We *can* "fall from grace." We can be earnest and grateful recipients of God's saving grace for a time—and then backslide.

This fact need not be discouraging, but it should be very sobering. There is no assurance of salvation that permits us to "rest on our oars." But since the choice is always ours, we *can* trust in God's love and press forward.

We do this best when our Christian experience is nourished in the fellowship of Christ's Church and when we are built up thereby in worship and service. So, in the next chapter we shall examine what the Church is and what God through the Church offers and requires of us for our growth in grace.

We Believe in the Church

*T*HE *Church is not essentially a human institution but is the community of believers of which
Jesus Christ is Lord and in which he works by
his Holy Spirit. It is the gift of God for the salvation
of the world through the proclamation of the evangel
of good news to all men. It asserts the claim of Christ
as the incarnate Word of God to the lordship of all
human life. It is universal in nature, standing greater
than any group claiming exclusively to represent it,
and above every nation and culture in which it finds
its home. Belonging to all the ages, it defies the passing
of the centuries and embraces within its visible and
invisible membership both the living and the dead.
Though composed of both human and divine elements, its nature is not abridged by the frailties of
those forgiven sinners who compose its membership. It is His body, the instrument of His active
power, and the bond of fellowship between all those
who accept His lordship.*

WHAT IS THE CHURCH?

The church is an established part of American life. There
are very few communities that do not have at least one church,
and the larger cities have many hundreds of them. Over sixty
per cent of the total population belongs to some religious
body. While church attendance by no means equals member-

ship, it is the regular and expected thing on Sunday mornings to find large numbers of people at church.

Life's most sacred moments are usually those of marriage, parenthood, and death. Even those persons but marginally connected with the church generally wish to be married by a minister or priest rather than by a justice of the peace. When death enters a home, the agency of the church is invoked, both for whatever comfort may be received and for a fitting funeral or memorial service. The baptism of the newly born is less common and varies according to different denominations, but it is still a widespread practice. So is the attendance of these same children, when they get a little older, at Sunday school. In short, to be connected with a church is not universal, but it is an established part of the American way of life.

But what more is it? The statement quoted above declares that it "is not essentially a human institution." This we believe. If it were not more than a human institution, it would not hold the place that it does in human society. The remainder of the chapter will attempt to define this "more" and to answer the question, What is the Church?

THE CHURCH AS THE COMMUNITY OF CHRIST'S FOLLOWERS

The Church is not essentially a human institution but is the community of believers of which Jesus Christ is Lord and in which he works by his Holy Spirit. It is the gift of God for the salvation of the world through the proclamation of the evangel of good news to all men. . . . Though composed of both human and divine elements, its nature is not abridged by the frailties of those forgiven sinners who compose its membership.

We have a great number of denominations in America—at least 250—and there are others in other parts of the world. In matters of detail in organization, practice, and grounds of authority, these many churches are by no means of one mind. While various factors, both theological and non-theological, cause divisions, the most basic cause for division lies in differing views of the nature of the Church. We cannot here go into all these differences. The more important fact is that amid divisions and differences there is a great unity. This centers in a common loyalty to Christ and the belief that God has commissioned the Church to carry Christ's gospel to all men.

Most, if not all, Christians believe that the Church is the community of Christ's followers and that in spite of its many weaknesses there is something of God's Spirit in it. They believe that it is meant by God to be universal and world-embracing. If a person believes this, he believes in the holy catholic Church.

Since we affirm this faith every time we repeat the Apostles' Creed, it may be useful to look a little further at this phrase, "holy catholic."

To call the Church holy does not, of course, mean that it is flawless, wholly divine, or something to be worshiped as God is worshiped. It is composed of people, and all people—even the most faithful Christians—have shortcomings. The Church, furthermore, is composed of people of varying degrees of faithfulness to Christ, and by no means are they all saints! Nevertheless, the Church is the perpetuator of a divine gospel. Its effectiveness is to be judged not by the strength of its organization or even by its numbers, but by its fidelity to this gospel.

In the Apostles' Creed the words "I believe in the holy catholic church" are followed immediately by "the communion of saints." The two phrases belong together, for the second explains the first. In short, the holy catholic Church *is* the communion of saints. But this may sound to modern ears like explaining the unknown by the more unknown! Therefore we ask, What is the communion of saints?

Communion means fellowship, literally a "strengthening together" of one another. A saint in Protestant thought is not a person canonized by the Church, nor is he the long-suffering martyr or the well-nigh perfect person he is often assumed to be. A saint in the New Testament sense is a faithful follower of Jesus Christ, a redeemed person who has found new life in Christ. A saint therefore means a Christian—a Christian who is particularly faithful to Christ. Paul's greetings "to all the saints in Christ Jesus" or "to the church of God which is at Corinth, with all the saints who are in the whole of Achaia" were sent to his fellow Christians who, in spite of difficulty, had managed by God's help to remain faithful.

Although we had better not tinker with the wording of the time-honored Apostles' Creed, we are perfectly justified in mentally substituting the words "the fellowship of the faithful." The communion of saints is the great company of Christian believers, past and present, living and dead, who have fought a good fight for Christ and who, in loyalty and devotion to him, have kept the faith. Some of these are still living; the greater number have entered into the higher, heavenly kingdom. Whether they are still in this life or have gone to God's nearer presence, they strengthen us. And in our flagging efforts to serve Christ we are spurred on by the thought of being "surrounded by so great a cloud of witnesses."

Such a community—or communion—is a human institution; but it is more than that, for it was established by the will and purpose of God, is sustained by the Holy Spirit, and seeks to exalt Christ "as the incarnate Word of God to the lordship of all human life." With this grounding and mission we have every right to call the Church *holy*. But what of its being *catholic?*

THE CHURCH UNIVERSAL

It is universal in nature, standing greater than any group claiming exclusively to represent it, and above every nation and culture in which it finds its home. Belonging to all the ages, it defies the passing of the centuries and embraces within its visible and invisible membership both the living and the dead.

The word "catholic" in the Apostles' Creed is written with a small "c" and does not mean *Roman* Catholic. It means something far more inclusive—Christ's universal Church of all denominations around the world. In a sense this is an ideal rather than an actual description of the churches, for Christ's body is broken by many divisions. A cynic is said to have remarked, "I believe in the Church universal and regret that it does not exist." Yet in another sense it is a very potent reality.

When we speak of the catholicity, or inclusiveness, of Christ's Church, we are affirming that it is world-embracing. The missionary outreach of the Christian gospel is implied in this fact. In our day and for the first time in its history, the Church has literally encircled the globe. This does not mean that the gospel has been "preached to every creature" but that there is no major part of the earth's surface where it has not in some measure been taken. From this it follows that we actually have a Church far more catholic than the early creed-makers could possibly have imagined.

The word "catholic" implies another matter of great importance. This is the fact that the Church was designed by God to be inclusive enough to embrace not only the people of all parts of the earth, but also persons of every race, color, nation, economic or social class, age, sex, culture, language, and station in life. Although churches have never fully lived up to this ideal and have often sadly departed from it, the Christian gospel has always been a rebuke to race prejudice, national or class conflict, and every other form of man-made division. Some of the issues in which "the fellowship of the faithful" have been most called upon to resist the world lie exactly at this point.

During recent years the term "ecumenical" has come into use to describe this inclusive unity or catholicity of the churches of Christ. The word means "from the inhabited world." It was used in the early centuries to designate the great councils such as the Council of Nicaea, to which representatives came from what was then the whole of Christendom—the section around the Mediterranean Sea where churches had been established. The term began to be used again in modern times after the great missionary conference at Edinburgh in 1910 had inaugurated movements to study the "life and work" and the "faith and order" of the Protestant and Eastern Orthodox churches. The Roman Catholic Church would be welcome in the ecumenical movement but prefers not to affiliate.

In the summer of 1937 at two historic world gatherings of Christians, the Conference on Life and Work at Oxford, England, and on Faith and Order at Edinburgh, Scotland, it was voted to merge these two movements to form the World Council of Churches. After some intervening stages, the World Council fully came into being at Amsterdam in 1948 and held its first great American meeting at Evanston, Illinois, in 1954. A third major assembly of the World Council of Churches meets in New Delhi in 1961.

Other expressions of the ecumenical movement are found in the International Missionary Council, which correlates the work of many denominational mission boards around the world, and in the United States we have the National Council of Churches and many state and local councils. Perhaps the most familiar form that the movement takes on the local level is the interdenominational observance of the World Day of Prayer on the first Friday in Lent by the women of many thousands of communities, not only of this country but in 144 countries of the world. It also comes home to us in the observance of World-wide Communion Sunday on the first Sunday of October in Protestant and Eastern Orthodox churches around the world.

The ecumenical movement, like the holy catholic Church from which it derives its authority and function, is not essentially an organization. It is a spirit that expresses itself in fellowship and mutual service. It is a fellowship of the faithful followers of Christ who see all men as brothers because God is our Father and who feel themselves knit together and mutually strengthened by a common loyalty to our Lord.

THE CHURCH AS THE BODY OF CHRIST

It asserts the claim of Christ as the incarnate Word of God to the lordship of all human life. . . . It is His body, the instrument of His active power, the bond of fellowship between all those who accept His lordship.

The most familiar symbolic term for describing the nature of the Church is a term coined by Paul. He used it repeatedly, and it was from the New Testament that it was taken over into modern diction. It is the phrase "the body of Christ."

This figure of speech is elaborated at length by Paul in the twelfth chapter of First Corinthians, where he compares the unity and interdependence of the members of Christ's Church to the interacting unity of the various members of the human body. Just as the foot needs the hand and the eye needs the ear, so the whole Church needs all its parts. As in the human body, even the weaker and less glamorous parts have their places. (Perhaps this was a subtle rebuke to the ecclesiastical prestige and clamor for position that was already emerging in the church of Paul's day!) The passage comes to a great climax in the words:

> If one member suffers, all suffer together; if one member is honored, all rejoice together.
> Now you are the body of Christ and individually member of it.[21]

[21] 1 Corinthians 12:26-27.

This same idea is repeated in Romans 12:4-8: "For as in one body we have many members, and all the members do not have the same function, so we, though many, are one body in Christ, and individually members one of another. Having gifts that differ according to the grace given to us, let us use them" for prophecy, for service, for teaching, for exhortation, for contributing, for giving aid, and for doing acts of mercy. Never have both our interdependence as Christians and the obligations stemming from diverse gifts and functions been better stated.

Yet the symbol of the Church as the body of Christ implies more than our mutual dependence and responsibilities, vital as these are. The Church is the body of which Christ is the Head. It must have no other head but Christ; the governing authorities and all else within it must be subject to him. It exists to exalt the lordship of Christ over all of life. When anything or anybody else becomes supreme, idolatry has corrupted its nature and distorted its function. Christ is the incarnate Word of God, and he alone must reign within it.

This is a requirement of the utmost urgency and is the ultimate test of whether or not our churches are really the Church. Wherever there is mere conventional attendance at or deference to the church; wherever there is self-seeking and clamor for prestige and power among either laity or clergy; wherever our service is becoming ingrown rather than outwardlooking; wherever, in short, there is conformity to the world instead of the proclamation and daily witness to the gospel that transforms the world, there Christ is dishonored and his lordship flouted.

To believe in the Church as the Body of Christ means many things. It means that there must be a missionary outreach to carry the gospel to many lands. It means that persons must witness to the gospel in a way that will make it relevant to the business, family, and social life of our day. It means the cancelling of all race distinctions within the Christian fellowship and, as soon as possible, within all community life.

It means better church schools and Christian schools of higher learning so that the heritage of our faith may be passed on more fully and vitally to oncoming generations and so that adults may understand more accurately the foundations of their faith. It means unremitting efforts to eliminate injustice, poverty, hunger, disease, and ignorance wherever they are found.

Such an effort is found in the sending of aid in the spirit of Christ to the victims of communist tyranny and to other persons made hungry and shelterless by war. Such efforts are also found in the earnest resolution to cement the bonds of brotherhood so that wars and fears of war may no longer devastate mankind.

"I believe in the holy catholic church, the communion of saints. . . ." Do *you?* Upon all of us who believe this, God lays the obligation to exalt the lordship of Christ and to justify our faith by our works.

10

We Believe in the Kingdom of God

*I*T IS *the reign of God in every department of
human society, the divine scale of values for
every individual, group, and nation. As Christian
perfection is the goal of the individual life, so is the
kingdom of God in human society. Its creation is a
co-operative task involving both God and man. The
pattern of a redeemed society is the thought of God.
Its achievement is through the spiritual energy imparted by His spirit in human hearts, but its final
consummation comes slowly through the joint efforts
of God and man, working side by side, in the struggle
to create a new and divine order and to make His
will be done on earth as it is in heaven.*

"THY KINGDOM COME. . . ."

Every time the Lord's Prayer is spoken, this petition is
uttered. What does it mean? Immediately it is followed by
the words, "Thy will be done, on earth as it is in heaven."
In a sense, these words must explain the meaning of the
Kingdom, just as the phrase "the communion of saints" explains the term "the holy catholic church." Yet this by no
means tells us all that we need to know about the Kingdom
and its coming.

Christians generally agree that the kingdom of God is the
central note in the teachings of Jesus. Parable after parable

deals with it. Glance, for example, at the thirteenth chapter of
Matthew, where the author of the Gospel has compiled a
number of parables that were doubtless spoken on various
occasions. We find there the parables of the sower, of weeds
growing in the wheat until the harvest, of the mustard seed,
of the leaven, of the treasure hid in a field, of the pearl of
great value, of the dragnet taking in all kinds of fish, of the
householder bringing out of his treasure what is new and
what is old. Others are found throughout all the Gospels.
Some like these are explicitly introduced with such words
as "the kingdom of heaven is like. . . ."; others, like the
stories of the good Samaritan (Luke 10:29-37) and of the
prodigal son (Luke 15:11-32), are related to the Kingdom
not by words but in substance. There can be no question
that to Jesus the kingdom of God, which is identical in meaning with the kingdom of heaven, is absolutely basic.

But what does the Kingdom mean? Jesus never specifically
defined it, for he was not a systematic theologian dealing
with precise distinctions in terms. He felt himself to be the
messenger of God to summon men to a life in God and
obedience to God, and definitions were farthest from his interest. He told us enough to build on, and a great call to
faith and love, to dedication, to service and pure living in
the midst of persistent evil, runs through all his teaching.
This unity is more important than any differences that emerge
as we examine his life and work.

Yet differences there were, and these differences make the
nature of the Kingdom the most disputed element in Christian theology. These differences stem mainly from the fact
that Jesus apparently accepted, though with some modifica-
tions, the apocalyptic ideas current in his time. Beginning
toward the end of the Old Testament period—notably in
the Book of Daniel—and growing in force through the inter-
Testamental era, the idea became prevalent that a heavenly
being would be sent from God to establish his reign among
his righteous followers. Thus with the condemnation of sin-

ners to eternal punishment God's kingdom would come suddenly and dramatically. This is suggested in the parables
of the weeds and of the dragnet referred to above (see Matthew 13:24-30, 47-50) and still more vividly in the "signs of
the end" found in the almost wholly apocalyptic chapters
Mark 13 and Matthew 24. There is an apocalyptic setting
also for three great parables in Matthew 25 which emphasize
watchfulness, fidelity, and brotherhood: the parables of the
wise and foolish maidens, of the talents, and of the Last
Judgment, in which our place in the Kingdom is to be determined by our service to our fellow men. Other incidental
references to a sudden end of this earthly regime are too
numerous to be overlooked.

The presence of these passages has caused a wide diversity
of views among both scholars and ordinary Christians as to
how the Kingdom will come. Will it come gradually or suddenly? On earth or only beyond earth? With Christ's visible
return or only as men accept him in their hearts? Will it come
in a gradually transformed society or only by the destruction
of the society we now have? Perhaps the most crucial of all
the questions is, Will it come by man's co-operation or only
by God's act? Quotations can be drawn from the Bible to
support all of these views.

We cannot in this brief presentation go into all the subtleties of this matter. It is the writer's view that Jesus did hold
to some aspects of the apocalyptic expectations of his time
and may have thought of himself as the heavenly being sent
by God to usher in a new order. But he also thought of himself as the Suffering Servant of God, a Messiah who would
conquer not by political power, as many of his contemporaries
hoped, or by dramatic and spectacular intervention, as the
apocalyptists expected, but by the long, slow process of winning men to faith in God and to the love of God and one
another. These notes became blended in his thought, but the
one that was uppermost in his message and which is rightly
dominant in ours is that which stresses trusting obedience

and suffering love and which is expressed in the way of the cross.

It is on this basis that we must now look further at the nature of God's kingdom.

THE NATURE OF THE KINGDOM

It is the reign of God in every department of human society, the divine scale of values for every individual, group, and nation. As Christian perfection is the goal of the individual life, so is the kingdom of God in human society.

Among divergent views of the Kingdom there is a common element in the belief that the Kingdom is the reign of God in a redeemed society. Christianity has never proclaimed a purely individual gospel. Often the major, if not the only, emphasis has been on the individual's receiving forgiveness of sins through the saving act of God, and this is often referred to as an individual gospel. Yet at least in the acceptance of the corporate fellowship of the Church, and usually, also, in some recognition of the Christian's obligation to serve his fellow men, Christianity has been a social religion.

The kingdom of God, whether thought of as that which gradually comes on earth through a transformed society or as that which comes only in God's eternal kingdom beyond death and earthly history, is always a social concept. Though it is personal in the sense that we can enter the Kingdom only by responding to the call and to the gift of God, we cannot enter or dwell in it alone. This is Christianity's answer to any kind of mysticism that centers in the solitary individual's confrontation and union with God. We must add, however, that the most creative and most prevalent forms of Christian mysticism are quite compatible with the idea of God's reigning in a redeemed society.

But what do we mean by a redeemed society? Do we have in mind one in which the outer structure is changed by legislation and the realignments of social institutions? Or are we referring to one in which the inner fabric is different? The answer is *both,* although the outer changes depend on inner reorientations for their motivation and strength. A society made over by totalitarian edict, as in much of the life under communism today, would not be the kingdom of God. But neither do we have the reign of God for the redemption of society when Christians are unconcerned about the plight of their fellow men, or when such giant evils as war, race discrimination, alcoholism, economic injustice, hunger and homelessness, and the shattering of family life go unchallenged. The Kingdom is "the reign of God in every department of human society."

And what *is* the reign of God? Does not God rule anyway? In an ultimate sense he does. This is our Father's world; he is not only "Maker of heaven and earth" but Ruler as well. This we ought never to forget in the midst of the world's evil. The suffering that comes in conjunction with the great social evils just mentioned is a persistent warning to us that God, the Ruler of all, requires us to make this earthly scene into the kind of world he wills it to be. Yet his rule must be accepted by men before this can happen. The Kingdom is God's design; man's disorder prevents its realization.

This conviction lies at the basis of the social gospel, which has sometimes been identified with the kingdom of God. More correctly, it is one expression of the Christian obligation to labor for the coming of God's kingdom. A redeemed society is one redeemed inwardly and outwardly, purged of personal sin and freed from the crippling and corrupting effects of social sin. It is a society redeemed for this life and for whatever in God's providence lies beyond our earthly destiny. Hence, it is not justifiable to identify the coming of the Kingdom with human social progress, but neither is it legitimate to overlook God's demand that in every aspect of human life our world must be fashioned more nearly to his will.

How Does the Kingdom Come?

Its creation is a co-operative task involving both God and man. The pattern of a redeemed society is the thought of God. Its achievement is through the spiritual energy imparted by His spirit in human hearts, but its final consummation comes slowly through the joint efforts of God and man, working side by side, in the struggle to create a new and divine order and to make His will be done on earth as it is in heaven.

We used to hear very often the phrase "building the Kingdom." It stood for a true emphasis that needs to be preserved, namely, the Christian's obligation to labor earnestly to do God's will on earth. But not only is the phrase itself unbiblical; it also has the unfortunate connotation that it is man, not God, who establishes the Kingdom. A .better metaphor is found in the parable of the sower: In Christ we sow God's seed and God gives the harvest.

In reaction to the activism and even the human presumption that was thought to underlie the idea of building the Kingdom through the social gospel, theologians in some circles have swung to the opposite extreme. There are eminent theologians today who refuse to admit that man has anything to do with the coming of the Kingdom. They regard its coming wholly as the act of God to take place in a final consummation when Christ comes again. This was brought sharply into the foreground by the discussions of the main theme of the Second Assembly of the World Council of Churches which met in Evanston, Illinois, in 1954. This theme was "Christ—the Hope of the World." Most Americans took this to mean that Christ is our hope both here and now and in man's future destiny on earth as in heaven. Many Europeans interpreted it as the hope of the coming of the Kingdom by God's act in a realm beyond earthly history.

The statement quoted above mediates between these extreme positions. "Its creation is a co-operative task involving both God and man." To say that "its final consummation comes slowly through the joint efforts of God and man" affirms, first, that there will be a final consummation; second, that we cannot expect it suddenly or catastrophically; and third, that the Kingdom comes only as God and man work together.

This statement is important in what it leaves unsaid as well as in what it affirms. Whether the final consummation will come on earth or only beyond earthly history, we do not know. That we must leave in God's hands. While sin remains, an earthly utopia is unlikely, and sin is not apt to be banished from the earth. Yet we must labor toward this goal. As we labor, sowing God's seed, it is unlikely that all of it will grow. There is always transiency and rootlessness, "the cares of the world and the delight in riches" to stifle fruitage. Yet some of our efforts will bear fruits. And though God gives the Kingdom, man must do his part. The "joint efforts of God and man, working side by side" should not be taken to mean equal partnership, for God is always Lord and we are his servants. Yet in the vision of God which Jesus gives us, the Lord of life is also Father and daily Companion.

Thus we come to this: that in the kingdom of God, God rules as Lord but loves as Father and works with us as Companion. Slowly, gradually, like the leaven and the mustard seed, the Kingdom comes as we labor faithfully in God's service. Some evidences of its coming we see about us in redeemed lives and in a better society; for others we must hopefully wait, labor, and pray. Christ comes wherever men accept him in faith and give him the dedication of their lives. And where Christ comes to take possession of men's lives, there the kingdom of God is manifest.

In a world cluttered with many interests and desires, anxieties and demands, there is one supreme obligation: to "seek his (God's) kingdom and his righteousness." When we do this, God's will is done on earth and his Kingdom comes. When we fail to do this, God's righteous judgment condemns us. At this, the sterner side of our faith, we must look in the next chapter.

11

We Believe in Divine Judgment

*G*OD *is not only the Creator but he is also the Judge of all the earth. All men and nations stand before His judgment bar. The moral law and the Christian ethic judge both sinner and saint. Beyond all human laws, customs, and opinions there is one divine Law which remains absolute and unchanging. Men may break themselves and their civilizations upon that Law but the Law itself stands forever. The judgments of the Almighty are true and everlasting.*

THE JUDGE OF ALL THE EARTH

One of the early stories recorded in the Book of Genesis has some searching words: "Shall not the Judge of all the earth do right?" (Genesis 18:25.) It is the story of the projected destruction of Sodom for its sinfulness, and Abraham protests that the Judge of all the earth will surely not slay the righteous with the wicked! Thus in one sentence both the judgment and the mercy of God are suggested. These two motifs are found throughout the Bible, and together they are imbedded in the Christian faith. To take away either is to withdraw from the other something vital and indispensable.

Yet God's mercy and judgment have not always been held in proper balance. The experienced fact of human sinfulness and the promise of salvation through the unmerited forgiveness of sin have placed much emphasis on divine judgment in traditional Christian thinking. Both the Old and New Testaments refer many times to the wrath of God. The apocalyptic passages in the New Testament also contain a number of statements of which this one at the conclusion of the parable of the weeds is typical: "The Son of man will send his angels, and they will gather out of his kingdom all causes of sin and all evildoers, and throw them into the furnace of fire; there men will weep and gnash their teeth. Then the righteous will shine like the sun in the kingdom of their Father." (Matthew 13:41-43.)

It is not surprising, therefore, that there developed very early a doctrine of heaven and hell with a sharp separation of the righteous from the wicked at death and the eternal punishment and torment of the latter. So deeply imbedded is this concept that, as was noted earlier, many people have trouble in thinking of salvation in any other terms than those of escaping hell and reaching heaven after death. They cannot conceive of it in any other fashion.

In recent years the belief in hell has waned among Protestants partly because of the difficulty of locating it in space but more from the conviction that a loving God would not want to condemn anyone—even a hardened sinner, to say nothing of a kind and highly moral person who is not a Christian—to endless torment. The ancient question "Shall not the Judge of all the earth do right?" leads us, as it led Abraham, to think that it would not be right for God to be so destructive.

As a consequence, we sometimes get too sentimental about the loving-kindness of God and forget that he is exacting as well as loving. The belief in a "fire and brimstone" hell we may well surrender; we shall say more about this later. But we cannot overlook the belief in divine judgment—and with it divine punishment—without distorting the Christian faith. So, what may we believe about it?

What Is Divine Judgment?

Divine judgment will be clearer, perhaps, if we think of it in terms of the justice of God. Both words are derived from the Latin *jus,* which means "right" or "law." A true judgment is passed when the decision reached is one that is right and just. We do not need to think of the judgments of God legalistically, as we do when a human judge instructs the jury in a court case; yet the judgments of God are directly related to the *laws* of God.

Likewise, we do not need to think of God's punishment as vindictive, retributive, or retaliatory. Our human tendency is to think of justice as "getting even," as one small boy strikes another and the other strikes back, or as a supposedly mature individual or nation thinks it must give back to enemies either the treatment received or something more severe. This ancient idea of the *lex talionis*—"an eye for an eye and a tooth for a tooth"—was explicitly repudiated by Jesus. But it still persists in our society even when our better sentiments recoil from it.

How, then, is punishment justified? Our best analogy is the human family, although even this must, of course, fall short of the infinite love of God. The child who is always indulged and never punished becomes a "spoiled brat" and grows up with less strength of character than one who is firmly and justly disciplined. Brutal or arbitrary punishment will not do; loving and just punishment is a necessity for the fullest achievement of character.

God is infinitely loving and just. He takes sin seriously, and all men are sinners. God would not be a God worthy of our worship—certainly not the God of Jesus—if he smiled indulgently upon our sins, bypassed them, and let us go on sinning with no evidence of divine disfavor.

The Hebrew prophets proclaimed again and again the judgment of God on a sinful nation. These words of Amos still ring in our ears:

Thus says the LORD:
"For three transgressions of Israel,
    and for four, I will not revoke the punishment;
because they sell the righteous for silver,
    and the needy for a pair of shoes—
they that trample the head of the poor into the dust
        of the earth,
and turn aside the way of the afflicted. . . ." [22]

Yet there is another side of this message—a note of hope in the midst of doom. Again we read the words of Amos:

Seek good, and not evil,
    that you may live. . . .

.   .   .   .

"I hate, I despise your feasts,
    and I take no delight in your solemn assemblies.

.   .   .   .

But let justice roll down like waters,
    and righteousness like an everflowing stream. . . ." [23]

Today, as in the eighth century before Christ, we find greed, exploitation, callous indifference to human need, and vast amounts of conflict and strife between nations and social groups. These situations always cause tension and suffering; sometimes they break out in war. But we must remember that these wars do not occur because God desires them. They take place because a just God has so ordered his world that sin inevitably brings suffering and distress in its wake. God respects the freedom he has imparted to his children and does not interrupt our sinning by any forced conformity to his will. But God the Judge is always the Ruler of his world.

There is a moral order in the world. When we break the laws of God, we are broken upon them. This does not al-

[22] Amos 2:6-7.
[23] Amos 5:14, 21, 24.

ways seem apparent in individual lives, however, for an obviously sinful person may seem to get along pretty well. Therefore we are inclined to ask Jeremiah's question,

> Why does the way of the wicked prosper?
> Why do all who are treacherous thrive? [24]

Yet inwardly there is a difference between the love, joy, and peace of the dedicated Christian and the person who demands more and more for himself in defiance of God and at the expense of other persons. Whether in a sense of guilt and inner unrest which drives many to psychiatrists or in the perhaps more terrible lethargy that drugs conscience to insensibility, punishment for unrepented sin is an inescapable fact of life.

Sometimes this judgment is interpreted as automatic punishment that goes on without God's concern simply because the world is made this way. But such a view of an inflexible moral order is not enough to express the full meaning of divine judgment. The personal God who punishes in love does not simply leave us to our own destruction. He yearns to save us, and his just condemnation never cancels his mercy. This is why he sent his Son, Jesus Christ, for our redemption, and this is the major message of our faith.

LAW AND GRACE

Beyond all human laws, customs, and opinions there is one divine Law which remains absolute and unchanging. Men may break themselves and their civilizations upon that Law but the Law itself stands forever.

Because all human laws, customs, and opinions change from time to time and vary from place to place, we tend to think of right and wrong as relative to the particular culture in which we live. To cite a familiar example, some Christians

[24] Jeremiah 12:1*b*.

think it is perfectly all right to drink a cocktail occasionally if they do not get drunk; others see this as a sin against God. Extend this dilemma to problems of family life and business dealings, to the moot problems of school integration and the use of atomic and hydrogen bombs in war, and it becomes evident that there is no unanimity among Christians as to the will of God in concrete matters of ethical decision.

When we look to the Bible for an absolute set of rules, we fail to find it. There are, to be sure, many sources of guidance in the Bible, but neither the Ten Commandments nor the words of Jesus tell us everything. If we take everything in the Bible literally as a mandate for today, we run into strange developments. For example, Deuteronomy 25:5 specified that if a man died without having a son, his brother must marry the widow and try to beget a son who would bear the dead man's name. And he had to do this regardless of whether or not he had a wife already! I do not know of any Christian in our time, however much of a biblical literalist, who feels obligated to keep this command.

Such factors may lead us into an ethical relativism regarding our duty as Christians. But ought this to happen? The statement quoted affirms that "there is one divine Law which remains absolute and unchanging." This is true and vitally important.

There is only one absolute and unchanging law laid for us by God through Christ. This is the law of love. Some would not call it a law, since love is not subject to command. But in any case, it is a supreme obligation. Jesus stated duties on which "depend all the law and the prophets" when he answered the inquiring lawyer's question with the words:

> "You shall love the Lord your God with all your heart,
> and with all your soul, and with all your mind. This
> is the great and first commandment. And a second is
> like it, You shall love your neighbor as yourself. . . ." [25]

[25] Matthew 22:37-39.

Under all circumstances, the Christian is obligated to do the most loving, serving thing he can. This will not always be the same thing under differing circumstances. Words that cut must sometimes be spoken if healing is to take place, while under other circumstances the same words would simply be unloving or even spiteful. Christians will not always agree as to what is the most loving course of action to take, as Christians today are not in agreement over participation in war. Yet love stands always as the one supreme Christian obligation.

And how is love related to justice? No end of theological and ethical writing has been done on this theme, and we cannot go into all the issues here. In brief, love and justice must be united, even as judgment and mercy are united in the nature of God. Love without justice becomes sentimentality; justice without love is no longer just, but vindictive. Then the coercive power that is a necessary instrument of justice replaces concern for persons. Many of the world's major tangles today stem from attempts to preserve justice by force without the love of neighbor which alone makes force justifiable. Apply this idea to the international scene, to labor disputes, to racial tensions, or to almost any other social problem, and it becomes evident.

This brings us to the idea of law and grace. Law is the instrument of justice, whether human or divine, although, as we have seen, there is only one supreme and unchanging divine law. Love is the expression of grace. The overflowing and, on our part, unmerited, love of God forgives our sin even though we still stand under the divine judgment, and the love of God for us enables us to love our neighbor. "We love, because he first loved us." (1 John 4:19.)

Amid the relativities and clashing opinions of our time, the law of God stands forever. It is a law that is more than law because its source is the grace of God. It is a justice that is more than judgment because it springs from divine mercy. From this fountainhead Christians are called to love all men as brothers and to treat all men with a justice that finds its criterion and springs of action in love.

After Death

The judgments of the Almighty are true and everlasting.

We come now to say a few words about that disputed subject, the reality of hell and the possibility of everlasting punishment meted out by God. Here opinions differ greatly among Christians, and anything we say must be tentative.

As we shall observe more fully in the next chapter, eternal life is a basic conviction of Christian faith. It is thought of in different ways, but this faith and hope are central in the faith of the Christian church. We do not know all about heaven because it lies beyond our observation and the Bible does not tell us all we should like to know. But most Christians believe that God provides such an eternal dwelling place for those who love him.

Eternal life in this affirmative sense, as indicated in the Gospel of John, is not simply continuance after death; it is a quality of life which begins here and is endless. Because this is true, can we not then assume that the rejection of the call to love and serve God lies also on *both* sides of death? Hell in this life is certainly a reality; there is no sufficient reason to think that it ends with death.

Hell must not be thought of as physical torment or endless burning in a sea of fire. This is pictorial imagery like the pearly gates and streets of gold with which heaven is often pictured. The basic ideas in the meaning of hell are alienation and separation from God by persistent rejection of him, the tighter forging of the chains of sin as we misuse our freedom, and the loneliness, remorse, and inner turmoil which are sin's worst punishment. It is unwarranted to suppose that the Judge of all the earth remits these penalties in life or beyond death if persons persistently and impenitently refuse his grace.

We have said that the wrath of God must not be taken to mean vindictiveness. It means God's inevitable condemnation and terrible judgment upon sin. It is because sin is so serious and divine judgment is so real that hell in the sense just indicated is a reality upon earth and may well be after death. God forces no man to love and serve him; but when we refuse his invitation, we bear the penalty.

Will all men after death eventually be won to acceptance? Some noted theologians think so on the ground that otherwise the redemptive purpose of the ever-loving God would be unfulfilled. Others, including the present writer, believe that human freedom is so basic to personality that its misuse in rejecting God's grace, whether in this life or the next, will always be possible. We do not know; we must leave this in the hands of a just and loving God.

"The judgments of the Almighty are true and everlasting" —yes, and righteous altogether. It is as good to be aware of these stern certainties as it is to have the equal assurance that in God's grace we shall find our peace.

12

We Believe in Eternal Life

MAN, whose earthly existence is so brief and uncertain, has nevertheless eternity set in his heart by the Creator. The words of Jesus and His resurrection from the dead bring to us the assurance that for the Christian death shall be swallowed up in victory. God is eternal, Jesus is the conqueror of the grave, and we, being united by faith with Him, share His everlasting life. Death is a doorway from a natural world into a spiritual world. Behind the thin veil that conceals from our human eyes the Blessed Country there stands One who has gone to prepare a place for us and who will one day receive us unto Himself in eternal glory. Heaven is the perfect companionship of the believer with Christ, and death is but a transition into the deeper fellowship of His nearer presence.

THE DIFFERENCE IT MAKES

"If a man die, shall he live again?" asked Job wistfully many centuries ago. This is still the query of our wistful, troubled generation. When our families and loved ones are in good health and things are going well, we may not think much about this subject. Then, too often, comes a sudden blow—an unexpected illness, an automobile accident, a telegram of "bad news" delivered at the door. Life has a way, sometimes in a moment, of sweeping away old securities and leaving us only God and our faith to stand upon. Job's question then becomes very real.

But suppose nothing of this sort happens. With minor ups and downs we may live out our "threescore years and ten" and—thanks to a good constitution and modern science—quite a few more. Has Job's question, then, any meaning? The one certain fact everybody confronts is that he must sometime die. The vigor of life will ebb and earthly ties will be severed.

> Twilight and evening bell,
> And after that the dark! [26]

sings the poet. And will there be dawn beyond the darkness? To this query our Christian faith gives a ringing and triumphant *Yes*.

There are some persons who say they do not care to live eternally and that they are not afraid to die even if it is a case of "after that the dark." This attitude, where it is honestly held, must be respected. But can we say this about separation from our loved ones when death removes them? Few can. Death is real; death is terrible; death without eternal life has a finality that severs our deepest ties and frustrates our best hopes.

The Christian faith in God's gift of eternal life obviously offers comfort and hope in the face of grief. It also offers challenge in the midst of life. If we are to live eternally, this life ought to be of such a quality that it provides a worthy beginning for that which is to come. According to John's Gospel, our Lord said, "Truly, truly, I say to you, he who hears my word and believes him who sent me, has eternal life; he does not come into judgment, but has passed from death to life." (John 5:24.) Though not all the noble living of the world is limited to Christians or to believers in eternal

---

[26] From "Crossing the Bar" by Alfred, Lord Tennyson.

life, there is a Christian conquest of death in the present life which is both a preparation and a foreshadowing of a greater conquest by God in the life to come.

But can we believe in eternal life? If so, let us see now on what grounds.

THE GROUND TO STAND ON

Man, whose earthly existence is so brief and uncertain, has nevertheless eternity set in his heart by the Creator. The words of Jesus and His resurrection from the dead bring to us the assurance that for the Christian death shall be swallowed up in victory. God is eternal, Jesus is the conqueror of the grave, and we, being united by faith with Him, share His everlasting life.

"How do we know?" is a common query. Many who would like to believe in eternal life have a rankling suspicion that it is a bit of wishful thinking intended to ease our loneliness and dread of dying.

Christians do not have the proof of eternal life in the same sense that we can prove a proposition in geometry or can verify a scientific theory. But this fact does not prevent us from having good and sufficient reasons for our faith. A faith it is, but a faith that fits in with all that we know about God and his goodness.

The first reason—and no other is really needed—is the Easter story. Let us imagine that we are a part of those great events that took place many years ago. On that fateful spring day in Jerusalem the first Good Friday must not have seemed very good to Jesus' followers. Their Leader was dead; was not his cause lost too? We read between the lines the despair of shattered hopes in the words, "We had hoped that he was the one to redeem Israel." (Luke 24:21.) With the earthly future so uncertain, eternal life and what he had said to them about it may well have been forgotten.

Then something happened! Early on the first Easter

morning, the women who loved him went to the tomb. There they learned that God was stronger than death.

Over my desk hangs a picture of Gutzon Borglum's "Mary Magdalene." The light of glad expectancy and new hope is in her eyes as she turns from the empty tomb to the living Christ. For her God's victory has conquered grief.

And so it was with the other disciples when this great, glad news was known. Again and again our Lord appeared to them until even Thomas could doubt no more. Gone were their frustration and despair. The little company was on fire with news they *had* to share. In this Resurrection faith the Church was born, and in its power the followers of the risen Christ witnessed to him in spite of persecution, pain, and death. We are the inheritors of that faith.

"Because I live, ye shall live also," was our Lord's promise. That is our first and best reason for believing in eternal life. But it is not the only reason. Both the goodness of God and the nature of persons, his supreme creation, point the way. This is not to say that we ourselves are good enough to deserve to be immortal! But God has made us "in His own image," not "like the beasts that perish." It is not reasonable to suppose that the God who made us and who loved us enough to give his Son for us would let us simply "go out" at death like snuffed candles in the dark. If the goodness and laughter, the faithful living, and the richness of soul in those we love seem precious to us, how much more that is worth preserving must God see in each of his children! The God who has set eternity in man's heart must think of man as destined for it.

WHAT IS HEAVEN LIKE?

Death is a doorway from a natural world into a spiritual world. Behind the thin veil that conceals from our human eyes the Blessed Country there stands One who has gone to prepare a place for us and who will one day receive us unto

Himself in eternal glory. Heaven is the perfect companion-
ship of the believer with Christ, and death is but a transition
into the deeper fellowship of His nearer presence.

It will not do for us to try to describe the next life too
precisely. There is much we should like to know yet shall
not know while we are on earth and while we "see in a
mirror dimly." But God has given us all the knowledge we
need. We know that we shall be in God's nearer Presence,
and that this will be joy. There is every reason to suppose
that we shall have fellowship with our loved ones. Perhaps
God will give us further work to do. Then our freedom from
bodily limitations that too soon cut off our usefulness here
will help us grow in the power to serve him better. If we
need some type of bodies to serve as vehicles of the spirit
there, God will give us what we need.

The Bible does not tell us a great deal about the nature
of the future life. The biblical writers knew, as we may know,
that it is the gift of God and that we can be safe in the
Father's hands regardless of its precise nature. In general,
they speak of it as resurrection, which emphasizes that it is
given by God's act and is not simply a natural endowment.
They also give us the idea that it is a new life under new
conditions, not simply a continuance of the soul when the
body dies. Some theologians today prefer not to use the
term "immortality" when they speak of the future life, lest
the Greek idea of the natural immortality of the soul be
suggested by it. But if "resurrection" is substituted as a
better biblical word, we must be careful not to assume a
resuscitation of these same bodies in which our spirits now
are housed. When these die, we are finished with them.

Paul used both terms, and in a marvelous statement found
in 1 Corinthians 15:35-58 he said as much about the nature
of the future life as can be said from this side of the veil. He
begins with a very simple but meaningful analogy—a grain of
wheat falling into the ground to die so that new life may come
from it. God then "gives it a body as he has chosen, and to

each kind of seed its own body." What follows can best be stated in Paul's own words:

> So it is with the resurrection of the dead. What is sown is perishable, what is raised is imperishable. It is sown in dishonor, it is raised in glory. It is sown in weakness, it is raised in power. It is sown a physical body, it is raised a spiritual body. If there is a physical body, there is also a spiritual body.
>
> .   .   .   .
>
> For this perishable nature must put on the imperishable, and this mortal nature must put on immortality. When the perishable puts on the imperishable, and the mortal puts on immortality, then shall come to pass the saying that is written:
>> "Death is swallowed up in victory."
>> "O death, where is thy victory?
>> O death, where is thy sting?" [27]

These words have a stirring challenge, a hope, and an assurance that never wear out. What the nature of the spiritual body is, or in what form "this mortal nature must put on immortality," we do not know. But what does this matter? God can be trusted to give us what he knows is best for us. There is so much in earthly existence that cannot be foreseen from one stage to the next as persons grow from infancy to childhood, to adolescence, to maturity, to old age, that it hardly seems wise to be too much concerned about what lies beyond.

So, without complete knowledge of what follows this life, millions of Christians through the ages have been enabled by a triumphant certainty to meet death without anxiety or fear. The words with which Paul closes the chapter from which we quoted may well be ours:

> But thanks be to God, who gives us the victory through our Lord Jesus Christ.

[27] 1 Corinthians 15:42-44, 53-55.

> Therefore, my beloved brethren, be steadfast, im-
> movable, always abounding in the work of the Lord,
> knowing that in the Lord your labor is not in vain.[28]

We noted earlier that one of our gravest concerns regarding this subject centers upon our loved ones who are taken
from us. Again and again our souls cry out, "Their going
would be endurable if we could believe we shall see them
again. *May* we believe this?" Why not, if what has been
said thus far is true? Though the Bible does not speak very
specifically on this question, it does have great words to
say about the kingdom of God; and the Kingdom, we saw,
is always a social concept. One of the greatest visions of
this coming Kingdom is found in the Book of Revelation,
where we read:

> There shall no more be anything accursed, but the
> throne of God and of the Lamb shall be in it, and
> his servants shall worship him; they shall see his
> face, and his name shall be on their foreheads. And
> night shall be no more; they need no light of lamp or
> sun, for the Lord God will be their light, and they
> shall reign for ever and ever.[29]

Pictorial language? Certainly. But it is imagery that suggests the joy of God's presence in a great fellowship
of which both we and our loved ones may constitute a part.
Furthermore, we may well believe that the God who has
made us for love and fellowship with one another here on
earth will not shatter this fellowship in the life beyond. It is
obvious that conditions and circumstances will be changed.
But love is stronger in death, and the love of God is stronger
than any human love. So why not trust him to reunite us
in this larger, more glorious life?

Eternal life means no solitary or static "going on" in

[28] 1 Corinthians 15:57-58.
[29] Revelation 22:3-5.

some bare existence devoid of meaning. If it were this, it would be hard to conceive that many would desire it. The Old Testament expresses an idea somewhat like this in what was called Sheol, which the King James Version incorrectly but suggestively translates "hell." Christian faith replaced it with a joy and a blessedness born of the revelation of the Father's love in Christ.

Eternal life for the individual person means hope in Christ, now and forever. It means that with this hope comes the challenge to service, certainly here and probably hereafter. "So faith, hope, love abide," said Paul. And, from all that we know, we have the right to believe that these will abide throughout eternity. Eternal life means also the triumph of God in a redeemed society as his kingdom comes both here and in a final victory beyond all time and space. This earth must certainly be important to God, but it is not all important. Human sin and strife might cause all human life to be annihilated, but still God would not be defeated. It is our Christian hope that Christ, who rose triumphant over sin and death, will reign forever in God's eternal kingdom and that we shall know the glory and blessedness of his presence.

The message of Easter, ringing through the centuries and around the world, is "Christ the Lord is risen!" As we respond in joyous faith and hope, let us entrust to him our loved ones and our lives and have no fear of death. He who said "Lo, I am with you always" will be our Companion and Guide, today and through eternity.

INDEX

Acceptance, 68
Acts, Book of, 26, 28
Alcoholism, 12
Amos, 110
Apostles' Creed, The, 92-94
Aristotle, 33
Atonement, 68
Augustine, 65
Authority, 23-24

Babcock, Maltbie D. (quotation), 15
Bacon, Sir Francis, 22
Barnabas, 26
Barth, Karl, 53
Bible, 42-51; as record of revelation, 43-45; as revelation of God, 80; as Word of God, 47; basis of faith and conduct, 45-47; criticism of, 48-51; guidance of, 112; King James Version of, 36, 49; Revised Standard Version of, 36, 49; view of man in, 56
Borglum, Gutzon, 119
"Breathe on Me, Breath of God" (poem), 44
Brunner, Emil, 53

Calvin, John, 88
Christ: see Jesus Christ
Christlikeness, 84-85
Church, 90-97; Body of Christ, 96-98; character of, 91-96; relationship to state, 43; divisions of, 92; faith of, 114; Holy Spirit in, 93; mission of, 97-98; revelation of God in, 80; unity of, 93.
Conversion, 67
Corinthians, First Epistle to the, 57, 68, 88, 96, 120-22
Corinthians, Second Epistle to the, 36, 40, 47, 67, 69, 75, 80
Criticism: biblical, 48-51; form, 50-51; historical (higher), 49-50; textual, 49
"Crossing the Bar" (poem), 117

Dead Sea scrolls, 51
Death, 87, 117-21
Deuteronomy, 112
Docetism, 27
Doddridge, Philip (quotation), 73

Ecumenical movement, 95-96
Ephesians, Epistle to the, 84
Episcopal Address of the Bishops to the General Conference of 1952 (quotations), 11, 18-19, 22, 25, 28-29, 32, 34, 39, 42-43, 45, 48, 52, 54, 56, 58, 60, 62, 65-66, 68, 72, 74, 76, 80, 82, 84, 86, 90-91, 93-94, 96, 99, 102, 104, 107, 111, 114, 116, 118-20
Eternal life, 114, 117-23
Evangelism, 78
Evil, 17, 55, 103
Experience, Christian, 72-81

Faith and Order, Second World Conference on, 95
Freedom, 17, 57

Gandhi, Mohandas, 30
Genesis, Book of, 15, 18, 54, 57, 107
God: activity of, 15-21; approach to, 25-26; as Creator, 15, 25, 37, 46, 55, 57, 103, 105; as Judge, 46; as Lawgiver, 25; as a Person, 18-19, 111; as Ruler, 15, 46, 103; as Trinity, 37, 41; attributes of, 18, 20, 109; belief in, 15-21; character of, 56; command of, 13; communion with, 19; Fatherhood of, 105; grace of, 38, 41, 85, 113, 115; image of, 18, 54-56; kingdom of, 99-105, 122; knowledge of, 23, 25; law of, 25; Lordship of, 105; love of, 19-21, 26, 30-31, 108; power of, 31; prayer to, 19, 47, 78-80; presence of, 33, 74, 79, 120; purposes of, 17-18; Spirit of, 51; reign of, 103; voice of, 26; wrath of, 115
Grace, 38, 41, 89, 115
Grace, relationship to law, 113

Hatch, Edwin (quotation), 44
Hell, 108, 114-15
The Higher Pantheism, 19
Holiness: see Perfection, Christian
Holy Spirit, 46, 74-75, 80-81, 86, 93; activity of, 80-81; descent of, 35; fruits of, 77; functions of, 33-41; in the Church, 35; gift of God, 40-41; nature and work of, 34-41; relationship to sanctification, 37-38; temple of, 57; witness of, 39; unity of with God in Christ, 40-41

Insecurity, 11-12, 15, 24
Integration (psychological sense), 68
International Missionary Council, 95

James, William, 76
Jeremiah, 111
Jesus Christ: and doctrine of Incarnation, 27; as our Guide, 28; as Head of the Church, 96-98; as man, 27; as Redeemer, 37; as revelation of God, 26, 30-31, 33, 46, 51, 80, 123; as the Truth, 25; belief in, 21, 25-31; Body of, 96-98; decision for, 65, 78, 87; Lordship of, 45, 93, 96-98; loyalty to, 76, 92-93; "mind of," 35; ministry of, 29; new life in, 30-31, 64, 93; Presence of, 31, 40; Second Coming of, 83, 101, 104; sinlessness of, 27, 37; Son of God, 26-27, 30, 46; spirit of, 98; teachings of, 28-29; victory over death, 29-31, 119, 123; wisdom of, 28; Word of God, 97
Job, 117
John, First Epistle of, 21, 113

124